Rutgers v. Waddington

LANDMARK LAW CASES & AMERICAN SOCIETY

Peter Charles Hoffer
N. E. H. Hull
Williamjames Hull Hoffer
Series Editors

For a complete list of titles in the series go to www.kansaspress.ku.edu

PETER CHARLES HOFFER

Rutgers v. Waddington

Alexander Hamilton, the End

of the War for Independence, and

the Origins of Judicial Review

UNIVERSITY PRESS OF KANSAS

Published by the University Press of Kansas (Lawrence, Kansas 66045), which was
organized by the Kansas Board of Regents and is operated and funded by Emporia
State University, Fort Hays State University, Kansas State University, Pittsburg State
University, the University of Kansas, and Wichita State University

Library of Congress Cataloging-in-Publication Data

Hoffer, Peter Charles, 1944– author.
Rutgers v. Waddington : Alexander Hamilton, the End of the War
for Independence, and the Origins of Judicial Review / Peter Charles Hoffer.
pages cm. — (Landmark law cases & American society)
Includes bibliographical references and index.
ISBN 978-0-7006-2204-7 (cloth : alk. paper)
ISBN 978-0-7006-2205-4 (pbk. : alk. paper)
ISBN 978-0-7006-2206-1 (ebook)
1. Rutgers, Elizabeth—Trials, litigation, etc. 2. Waddington, Joshua—Trials,
litigation, etc. 3. Military occupation damages—New York (State)—New York—
History—18th century. 4. United States—History—Revolution, 1775–1783—
Claims. 5. United States—Foreign relations—Law and legislation—History—18th
century. 6. Treaty-making power—United States—History—18th century.
7. Hamilton, Alexander, 1757–1804. I. Title.
KF228.R877H64 2016
346.74703'6—dc23
2015035635

British Library Cataloguing-in-Publication Data is available.

Printed in the United States of America

10 9 8 7 6 5 4 3 2 1

The paper used in this publication is recycled and contains 30 percent postconsumer
waste. It is acid free and meets the minimum requirements of the American National
Standard for Permanence of Paper for Printed Library Materials z39.48-1992.

CONTENTS

In recent decades, a great deal of attention has been devoted to ending conflicts in societies through various methods of reconciliation. World War II ended with a victor's peace that included occupation and criminal tribunals in both the former Nazi Germany and the Empire of Japan. The fall of communism in Eastern Europe and the effective end of the Cold War led to efforts, not always successful, to stitch back together the quilt of civil society after decades of suspicion, informants, and secret prisons had sown deep divisions of distrust. At the end of apartheid in South Africa, they created reconciliation commissions. So, too, did our founding fathers attempt to find rapprochement between the previously warring factions of Americans, Revolutionaries and Loyalists, in the decade that followed the bloody birth of our nation.

Peter Charles Hoffer, through the little-known but remarkable legal case of *Rutgers v. Waddington*, recounts for us a tale of political and constitutional intrigue involving some of the most important actors in the transitional era from a confederation of states under the Articles of Confederation to a national republic under the U.S. Constitution. Appearing for the defendants was war veteran, future Federalist, and first secretary of the treasury, Alexander Hamilton. And, as always, lurking in the background was the estimable Aaron Burr.

It is also the story of a location as much as it is about the litigants and their lawyers. New York City is not just the setting for this landmark law case. It is a character in the drama that unfolds. While not representative of the Chesapeake, the Deep South, or New England, New York City had its own substantial role to play in the history of the republic, just as it had in the colonial period and the revolution. Then, as now, it was a center for commerce, a mix of ethnicities and nationalities, divided not just by faction and loyalties, but class and interest. Hamilton and the other lawyers of the city served their clients, but they also represented the divisions in their city. In so doing they paved the way for its future.

Hoffer's *Rutgers v. Waddington* thus illustrates a foundational moment in the young nation's history. As such, it is an encapsulation of a society riven by war and buffeted by revolutionary change, attempting to piece together the true meaning of "rule by law, and not by men" as John Adams so fittingly described it.

When does a revolutionary war end? When the guns are silent? When the peacemakers have finished their labors? When fundamental change has run its course? When a rule of law replaces a rule of violence? When a new order of law and governance is established? All of these questions can and should be asked of the American War for Independence, at least insofar as it entailed a constitutional upheaval. For the most noteworthy facet of the American Revolution was its replacement of colonial charters in an imperial system with republican constitutions for sovereign states. The war was fought to protect those new legal institutions. Under these fundamental laws state legislatures fashioned statutes for the victors and the vanquished. But so long as an iniquitous distinction was made between Patriot and Loyalist, native and visitor, there could be no real end to the war. Only when the Loyalists were reincorporated into the body politic and foreigners' rights protected did the War for Independence, as a legal event, truly come to a close.

One way to achieve these ends lay in the law courts, where Patriot lawyers defended the rights of British citizens and former Loyalists. Between 1783 and 1789 a cadre of young, able, and spirited American lawyers undertook this task. But they did not view that task in isolation from wider political and economic issues. They saw in the successful defense of these suits both a restoration of America's place in the world of Atlantic commerce and the basis for a truly national polity and economy. They practiced law locally but thought globally, and their thinking fostered a robust federalism.

The most important case in this category is the New York lawsuit *Rutgers v. Waddington* (1784). Rarely given proper attention, *Rutgers* is invariably treated as a small part of something else—a forerunner of judicial review; a proof that the new nation adopted international law; as Hamilton's breakout legal case; and as the capstone case in the Mayor's Court, to name four. *Rutgers* was all of these things, but it was more. It represented the end of the legal wars of the American Revolution and the beginning of the transformation of a weak confederation into a strong federal system.

It may seem odd to regard a law case as signaling a war's end—but not so strange if one recalls the close relationship between war and law in the eighteenth century. The great international law-of-war treatises of the seventeenth and eighteenth century, particularly Emmerich Vattel's *Law of Nations*, were as much about law as they were about war. European and American wars of the eighteenth century ended with treaties—legally binding documents arrived at not alone by violent means, but by negotiation. Prussian general Karl Von Clausewitz's infamous adage that war is the continuation of diplomacy by other means requires a coda—that legal settlements are the continuation of war by other means. *Rutgers v. Waddington* lay in the penumbra of one of these wars, the War for American Independence, and the legal arrangements which followed, the Peace Treaty of Paris of 1783 and the fabrication of the federal Constitution.

It is not quite so odd to argue that law cases can foreshadow the future. In a system of common law, every case can become precedent, controlling the outcome of cases to come. *Rutgers* was not a Supreme Court case like so many in the Landmark Law Cases and American Society series. It did not command obedience from later courts. But it was a reference point, a vital way station on the road to judicial independence, that lawyers and judges in later years recognized.

All law cases are transitional—they rest upon what has gone before (especially in our system of precedent) and harken to what will come. But some cases in our history are more than transitional. Landmark cases are transformative. They change the way the game is played, the rules by which it is played, and elevate the players to fame. The importance of *Rutgers* has been overshadowed by the Revolution that preceded it and the constitutional reforms that followed it; reexamined in its historical context *Rutgers* reveals itself as one of those transformative cases.

As an event in our history, *Rutgers* looked backward to a time of civil war in America and forward to a time of more permanent union. In 1784, the United States of America was a confederation of independent and sovereign republics. History taught the revolutionary generation that such arrangements had always ended in swift decline and violent dissolution. The signs foretelling this fate for the newly fashioned United States of America were already ominous—

grumbling unpaid veterans; divisions among western farmers and eastern creditors; trade wars between states; a failing diplomacy; and a confederation too weak to pay its debts, defend its borders, or even keep peace among contending land development companies. The briefs and the opinion in *Rutgers* hinted that a different fate could be had if different laws were adopted. These, in the form of a stronger national union, already percolated in the minds of key players in the litigation.

Returning *Rutgers* to its time and place raises a corollarial set of questions for students of the early national period. The notion that the federal Constitution was a kind of counterrevolution, a backing away from the more radical aspects of the Revolution, has long intrigued American historians. If one accepted some version of this theory, one might regard *Rutgers* as hinting at the beginning of the counterrevolution. The argument that property rights derived from the state (the plaintiff's case in *Rutgers*), countered by the argument that property rights derived from the nation and its treaty obligations (the defendant's response), might then be viewed as a microcosm of the larger dispute between the antifederalists and the federalists in 1787. At the same time, even the most consistent and persistent advocates of this view—men like Alexander Hamilton—did not see their efforts to create a stronger national government and a more business-friendly economy as a counterrevolution. They thought they were saving the Revolution and the new nation from disunion, disorder, and destruction.

———

All historical scholarship revisits subjects and places that earlier generations of historians have explored. Each new generation of historians stands on the shoulders of its predecessors. Ideally, more recent works contribute new and more perceptive readings of old documents and events. Much of the following story will be familiar to those of my colleagues who specialize in early national American history and law. Hopefully some of the insights here will be new and welcomed, if not immediately accepted, by them. The purpose of this essay, however, lies in another place. My aim is to bring to life for lay readers and students of history a world of law that we have lost, and a time when the fate of the nation may well have lain in the hands of its lawyers.

I am grateful to the David Library of the American Revolution, the New-York Historical Society, and the libraries at the University of Georgia, the University of Georgia School of Law, Rutgers Law School, Camden, the New York University Law School, and the University of Pennsylvania. Permission to use the Colonial Office Records for New York, the Burr Papers, the Guy Carleton Papers, and the Philip Schuyler Papers at the David Library, and the Egbert Benson, Richard Varick, and James Duane papers at the New-York Historical Society is herewith acknowledged. Oxford University Press graciously allowed me to revisit portions of my *For Ourselves and Our Posterity: The Preamble to the Federal Constitution in American History* (2013), 51–58, for the present essay.

Benjamin Carp, Dan Coenen, Daniel Hulsebosch, and David Konig were kind enough to agree to read the manuscript for the author. I am grateful. N. E. H. Hull, a long-time collaborator, read the manuscript and spotted stylistic and factual errors. My debt to her can never be fully repaid. Chuck Myers was a model editor in both senses of the word—reading the manuscript as a friendly referee and shepherding it through the adoption and production process. Kate Brown and Mark McGarvie read the manuscript for the press and offered immensely helpful suggestions. Remaining errors are, of course, my own.

Rutgers v. Waddington

Introduction

Of Hamilton and a Brewhouse

Sometime in the last days of winter 1784, twenty-nine-year-old attorney Alexander Hamilton surely stopped to contemplate the ruins of the Rutgers family brewhouse on Maiden Lane, between William Street and Pearl Street in Lower Manhattan. Romantically crafted classical and gothic ruins called "follies" were a fad in wealthy Englishmen's landscape gardens, but the brewhouse's condition would hardly have stirred anyone's sentimental attachment. Once a substantial establishment, now gutted by fire and abandoned for half a year, of the former substantial malt-house and ovens, only the firewood shed and the stables still stood. The property had value because of its location, but if past costs of repair were any indication, it would take nearly £1,000 (about $150,000 in twenty-first-century money) to bring the brewhouse back into operation and, if desired, establish a retail business in the complex. Still, Hamilton must have appreciated what the brewhouse represented, because he was now involved in a case concerning back rent for it. It was not a case that would make or break his still-new legal practice. Business was picking up and he had other clients. But if he won—when he won—he would move into the top tier of counselors in the city. That was his goal, but only the start of his ambitions.

Brewing was big business in the colonies and new nation. Beer and cider were the common potables of the day. Well water was dangerous unless boiled (hence the rage for stimulants like tea and coffee among those who could afford these imports). The facilities of a brewhouse were capacious—a manufacturing plant and a wholesale operation required great vats for mixing, a hot water supply, storehouses, woodsheds, barrels for fermenting and distribution, access to the streets for deliveries, as well as retail space if a tavern was attached. A whole block was not an unusually large accommodation. Although imported rum, fortified wines, and hard liquor like gin rivaled beer consumption, and more cider was consumed by volume than beer, no colonial town of any size was without its brew and malt houses.

One might even say that breweries enabled and defined New York City public life. Without the brewery, there would be no taverns. Without the tavern, the social life of the city would be bereft. Taverns were public spaces where rich and poor gathered. Politics was a major topic of the patrons, along with common gossip, business dealings, and other social intercourse.

Breweries appeared early in the Dutch city of New Amsterdam, to the consternation of Dutch West India Company Director Peter Minuit. He feared—rightly if one believes contemporary accounts—that public drunkenness made the city nearly ungovernable and opened it to attacks from Indians and European rivals. Still, his successor director, Wilhelm Kiefft, allowed the sale of liquor in the same building as housed his government office. By the eve of the Revolution the city had over twenty breweries.

New York was not alone in its embrace of tavern life and intoxicating beverages. City growth and tavern proliferation went hand in hand. Eighteenth-century Philadelphia, the largest colonial city, featured a "brewers' alley" on Wood Street, between Ninth and Tenth. The city had over thirty breweries. Even one of its mayors, Anthony Morris II, owned a tavern. Benjamin Franklin's *Poor Richard's Almanack* featured a variety of recipes for malts adaptable for brewing. In Boston, Samuel Adams inherited his father's successful malt house but ran it into the ground.

Despite hosting dozens of breweries, the officials of colonial New York City, Philadelphia, and other cities and towns railed against the ills of public drunkenness. Although beer was considered less dangerous than consumption of gin or other more alcoholic intoxicants, the amount of consumption was enormous. Colonial legislatures responded by regulating the licensing of brewhouses, along with the taverns and ordinaries they supplied—the proliferation of laws serving as ironic testimony to their general ineffectiveness. William Livingston, as close to an aristocrat as one could come in New York City (he was the younger brother of Robert Livingston, proprietor of the Livingston Manor, about whom more shortly), entertained readers of his *Independent Reflector* with a description of the "idle, drunken snorers" who made up the city watch and the "low, profligate, drunken, and faithless" workers whose misconduct the city watch was supposed to curb. The dangers public inebriation posed did not stop with tipplers' disorderliness. Even the elite were irresponsible when under the influence. It was said that Oliver DeLancey, one of the city's merchant captains, killed a man in a tavern brawl. His brother James was a notorious alcoholic.

Fire was another hazard breweries brought to the city. Not only was the storage of alcoholic beverages an invitation to accidental fires, breweries used wood-fired ovens to process the hops, malt, and other grain ingredients into a semi-liquid sugary mash. Cinders and ash wind-blown from the brewery and landing on the wooden roofs of the city could cause fast-spreading conflagrations. The disastrous New York City fire of September 21, 1776, did not consume Rutgers's brewhouse but might well have been the result of another brewery's carelessness. Similar establishments were the cause or the victim of many an eighteenth-century urban conflagration. The calamitous Boston fire of 1760 began in a tavern. Robert Hare's brewhouse in Philadelphia produced George Washington's favorite porter, a beer variety, until the structure burned to the ground.

––––––––

Ten years earlier, teenaged Hamilton had regularly passed the Rutgers family brewhouse on the way from his lodgings near the East River to Kings College, overlooking the Hudson River. The college hall was a busy and imposing structure and he was a scholarship student there. We do not know if during these walks he dropped in to a tavern to imbibe or listen to the locals talk about how they would teach Parliament a lesson. We do know that Hamilton stood not far from this spot in 1774, speaking spontaneously to a protest meeting, urging solidarity with the Tea Party rebels in Boston. Hamilton's oration brought cheers and applause from the assemblage and marked the beginning of his public career.

Hamilton's appearance that day, like his role in the coming of the

Revolution, owed a great deal to coincidence. He was not a native of the city or even of the mainland colonies. He was born in 1757, on the West Indian island of Nevis, to a Scottish merchant and ne'er do well named James Hamilton and a local Huguenot woman, Elizabeth Faucett. The family was not wealthy but owned several slaves and a homestead. Hamilton's prospects should have been reasonably bright, but his father deserted the family and his mother died when he was young. Hamilton was reared by the kindness of strangers, a collection of Presbyterian worshippers, Jewish philanthropists, and overseas traders. Restless himself, ambitious and brilliant, and an autodidact like Benjamin Franklin, the teenaged Hamilton found passage to the mainland as a supercargo on a merchant vessel. It is not clear whether he had been promised a place at the College of New Jersey, but when an offer did not materialize Hamilton enrolled at King's College in the City of New York.

Young Hamilton was at ease with both the brawling street politics and the sophisticated political polemics of the protest. His energy and fierce commitment marked him as a young man to be watched by both sides in the controversy. Though he never liked or trusted the crowd, and at first he supported the crown (owing his place at the college to its Loyalist president Myles Cooper), Hamilton was soon writing pamphlets defending the Continental Congress. On December 14, 1774, readers were treated to an early example of the forcefulness of his prose: In *A Full Vindication of the Measures of Congress*, Hamilton wrote, "It was hardly to be expected that any man could be so presumptuous as openly to controvert the equity, wisdom, and authority of the measures adopted by the Congress—an assembly truly respectable on every account, whether we consider the characters of the men who composed it, the number and dignity of their constituents, or the important ends for which they were appointed."

Despite the demands of college coursework and the effort required to turn out his pamphlets, there must have been time for visits to taverns. The literary club to which he belonged met in watering spots close by the college, as did the various loosely affiliated blocs of rebels calling themselves Sons of Liberty. Hamilton must have met some of the latter. Throughout the crisis, Jasper Drake's tavern near the college was a gathering place for Sons of Liberty. Family connections mattered to political allegiances. Drake was Isaac Sears's father-in-law, and Sears was a leader of the Sons of Liberty. There and in other taverns Patriots met to plot their resistance to the crown, consuming gallons of intoxicants in the process of what one historian has aptly called "tavern sociability."

The Sons of Liberty in New York and Boston were apprentices and master craftsmen, shoemakers, tailors, and dockworkers, along with a somewhat more shadowy cadre of the better sort, like Boston's Samuel Adams. A good number of these men's families, like Drake and Adams, held liquor licenses from the colonial governments. New York City's license holders included the extended Rutgers family. The property on Maiden Lane had passed down through the generations of Dutch New York Rutgers brewers to the widowed Elizabeth Rutgers and her sons.

Taverns became the targets of British forces during the crisis. The Rutgers brewhouse survived a 1770 brouhaha between British troops quartered in the city and John Lamb's Sons of Liberty. Lamb and his crew erected a liberty pole to embarrass the British. When at first unable to pull down the pole, the troops took out their animus on Montayne's Tavern, the Sons' hangout nearby. Four years later, a broadside from the British ship of war *Asia* replied to the protestors' mobbing of departing British troops by sending a cannon ball through Fraunces Tavern's roof. Sons of Liberty had planned the mob action in that very tavern. The Rutgers brewhouse escaped the fire of September 21, 1776, when half the city burned.

Hard times fell on the Rutgers brewhouse when the British forces drove the Revolutionaries from the city in late summer 1776, however. The widow Rutgers and her sons fled before the British forces appeared, leaving behind buildings stripped of everything save a cistern full of holes and a few pipes. British army regulars, never known for their respect for private property, were quartered in the brewhouse until 1778. In that year the commissary general, Daniel Weir, a civilian official acting under the authority of the military governor of the City (not the British quartermaster general, a serving officer whose primary duties were military), General William Howe, licensed British merchants Benjamin Waddington and Evelyn Pierrepont to reopen the brewhouse. Joshua Waddington, a British subject and a resident of New York, Benjamin Waddington and Evelyn Pierrepont's agent, oversaw the rebuilding of the brewhouse at the cost of £700 and leased it to tenants. In 1780, the new military governor of the city, General Henry Clinton, arranged for the leaseholders to pay a yearly rent of £100 pounds sterling for the use of the poorhouse. The tenants paid that amount until March, 1783, when the tenants departed and the building was once again vacant. A fire of mysterious origin gutted the structure in November, 1783, and set off the lawsuit that would become a national cause célèbre.

Hamilton's role in the unfolding story of *Rutgers v. Waddington* is well known. Another New York lawyer of Hamilton's close acquaintance also belongs in the story, though his presence has never been given its proper attention. Aaron Burr did not take up the cause of the widow Rutgers, but he represented many like her in the Mayor's Court. The two men both competed for clients in the city and state courts and joined forces when clients wanted both of them. Burr looked on as Hamilton made his case in *Rutgers*, no doubt impressed and a little envious, for the case enhanced Hamilton's reputation as a lawyer. Burr's shadow then fell over the aftermath of the case, as he and Hamilton jockeyed for political office in the state, and then in the new nation, a rivalry that turned menacing with the passage of time.

The First American Civil War

In 1765, New York City was the second largest city on the British North American mainland. Its upwards of 16,000 men, women, and children occupied a patchwork of wards. Some of these neighborhoods featured streets of townhouses, the urban mansions of the day, while others were crisscrossed with lanes of homes and workshops of artisans. Meaner alleyways were cluttered with the hovels of the working poor. On the street English, Scottish, Welsh, German, French, Portuguese, and African mingled. The wars for empire between the French and British had brought to the City high rates of employment and the opportunity for riches to everyone from silversmiths to thieves. Warehouses bulging with consumer goods along the East and the North (Hudson) Rivers were targets for criminal rings. From one of the waterside taverns had come the conspiracy of 1741, an uprising of slaves concealing a burglary ring of whites and blacks that would have burned a good part of the City to cover their activities. The waterfront was the notorious home of prostitution as well, a relief to the swelling numbers of seamen and a headache to the corporation whose mayor and aldermen ran the City—or tried to. Enforcement of the laws was left to the criminal courts, informants, the watchmen, and the victims themselves.

The City government, corporate in form, regulated wages, prices, and fees, down to the composition of the roofs of new buildings (slate instead of flammable wood) and the military stores that the British forces stockpiled in the city (for the city was the headquarters of British forces on the mainland). The presence of the British empire was everywhere apparent in a myriad of royal officials. Local magistrates, called justices of the peace, held commissions from the crown. The highest of officials, the royal governor, could call for elections, name the members of the council (the upper house of the legislature), and choose the judges of the colony's courts.

With the end of the French and Indian War, in 1763, good times disappeared for the majority of City folk. The very rich did not feel the pinch quite so hard, but bad crop years, the end of the British military spending, and spiraling inflation devastated the poor. The City was treated to a return of the "rough musick" (the contemporary term for rioting) that in past years had targeted houses of ill repute, greedy merchants, and foreigners. This time it was aimed at the British government. New York City was not the birthplace of the protests against Prime Minister George Grenville and parliamentary impositions like the Sugar Act of 1764 and the Stamp Act of 1765. But in the summer and fall of 1765, New York's Sons of Liberty brought the protests begun in Boston to New York City. Lieutenant Governor Cadwallader Colden and General Thomas Gage, commander of His Majesty's troops in North America, could only watch as the Sons of Liberty marched down Broadway with torches and effigies of parliamentary leaders. The stamped paper required by the Stamp Act was never distributed and Parliament rescinded the act. Later protests against the Townshend duties in 1767 and the Tea Act in 1770 brought protesters to the streets again, as the City became a stage for local resistance.

Street politics undermined the deference that the lower orders had, in earlier days, paid to their betters. Now the political world, if not quite turned upside down, had tilted to the left. The Sons of Liberty were organized by men of the "middling" sort and supported by laborers of the lower class. Wine merchant John Lamb, mariner Isaac Sears, and importer Alexander McDougall were its leaders. Not all roughnecks, but by no means gentry, such men became the backbone of the protests, holding meetings, distributing broadsides, plotting and mobilizing street demonstrations. While they did not call for democratic reform, much in their vocabulary of rights and wrongs and their style of politicking hinted at the more inclusive and popular politics of the next century.

The great mercantile and landed families in the colony could not ignore the street politics of men like Lamb, McDougall, and Sears. High-status merchants like Oliver DeLancey and politicians like James DeLancey initially supported the protests against the Stamp Act and in return gained the votes of the Sons of Liberty. But opportunities that only the favor of imperial officials could provide led the DeLancey family into the pro-British camp by the eve of open hostilities. Farther up the Hudson, aristocratic families like the Livingstons contested control of the colonial assembly with the DeLanceys. When the DeLanceys chose the British side in the quarrel with Parliament, the Livingstons moved to cement an alliance with the Sons of Liberty.

It was an odd pairing. With estates amounting to 250 square miles spread along the eastern shore of the river, "manor lords" like Robert Livingston had little in common with men like Lamb. The Livingstons treated their hundreds of tenants with a studied disdain. But the Livingstons decided that they could best protect their holdings in the colony by joining the protest against Parliament. Back and forth, the contest of great families and alliances across class boundaries fed into and off of the crisis.

None of the members of these leading families, any more than the spokesmen for the Sons of Liberty, could have predicted that a war for independence was on the horizon or that it would force everyone to choose sides, but the momentum of the protests was almost unstoppable. When New York's Patriots learned that Parliament would close the port of Boston to punish that city's Sons of Liberty for the "tea party" of December 16, 1773, protest resolutions from the various counties promised support for Boston. As one from Tryon County warned,

> the Act for blocking up the port of *Boston* is oppressive and arbitrary; injurious in its principles, and particularly oppressive to the inhabitants of *Boston*, whom we Consider brethren suffering in the common cause . . . we will unite and join with the different Districts of this county, in giving whatever relief it is in our power to the poor distressed inhabitants of *Boston*; and . . . we will join and unite, with our brethren of the rest of this Colony, in any thing tending to support and defend our rights and liberties.

The protests made New York's royal governor William Tryon's rule untenable and Loyalists' protestations of allegiance dangerous. As one anonymously authored handbill appearing in the City on September 14, 1774, warned, "After these laudable examples of the merchants and tradesmen of this city, there is no doubt but their patriotick conduct will be followed by all their fellow-citizens. But notwithstanding, should any sordid miscreant be found amongst us, who will aid the enemies of this country to subvert her liberties, he must not be surprised if that vengeance overtakes him, which is the reward justly due to parricides."

For a time the Patriot elite in the colony resisted turning full control of the protest over to the "mechanicks" whom Lamb and his colleagues led in the streets. When the call went out for delegates to a continental convention to meet in Philadelphia in May 1774, a hastily assembled committee of fifty-one selected delegates Isaac Low, John Jay, Philip Livingston, James Duane, and John Alsop. All but Low were lawyers, and all represented the interests of important families in the colony. All would later play important roles in the legal affairs of the new state, save Low, who became a Loyalist. With hostilities looming, the Committee of Fifty-One was replaced on November 22, 1774, by a Committee of Sixty, more radical and more inclined to overthrow British rule than its predecessor. The committee called for elections to a Provincial Congress for the colony that amounted to an alternative government, casting off the colonial assembly, council, and governor. On May 1, 1775, a Committee of One Hundred succeeded the Committee of Sixty and set about ridding the countryside of Loyalists—while still insisting that the protest did not amount to severing the ties with Britain. In effect this shadow government made reconciliation with the British authorities almost impossible, even had the British been inclined to seek it.

Despite the protests, no one among the Patriot party called for independence. Elite Patriot politicians were concerned that a demand for independence would bring war, and war would unleash the mischievous potential of the lower classes. To this extent they were right: when independence was finally declared, committees of safety composed of men of ordinary means roamed the interior of the state demanding that heads of households sign loyalty oaths. More than 80 percent of the men in the colony ascribed to the oaths, but long-time and much beloved Livingston allies like William Smith Jr. had no choice but to seek shelter in the City and take oaths of loyalty to the crown. Moderation and neutrality vanished.

In making such decisions, personal connections mattered more than ideology. James Duane, a lawyer for the Livingstons, had more in common with William Smith Jr. than with Sears or Lamb. Both Duane and Smith had little faith in the leadership capacity of the demos. John Jay, another of the Livingston intimates, was by temperament not inclined to street politics, much less to provoking bloodshed. As he and Duane tried to decide how to proceed in the months before independence, they weighed "all the horrors of a civil war" against the rights of the colonists. As Jay wrote to his brother at the end of 1775, "Though we desire reconciliation, we are well prepared for contrary measures."

In the meantime, the Committee of One Hundred and committees of safety in the countryside made suspected Loyalists' lives unpleasant. "The violent spirit [of the Patriots] . . . in harassing and oppressing the loyal," according to Church of England minister Richard Mansfield, drove him to abandon his flock and parish in the countryside and flee to the City. In September 1774, the Reverend Samuel Seabury, writing under the pseudonym "The Westchester Farmer," explained how difficult it was for Loyalists to stay at home when the committees of safety raged over the land. "Choose your committee, or suffer it to be chosen by half a dozen fools in your neighborhood, open yours doors to them, let them examine your tea canisters and molasses jugs, and your wives and daughters' petticoats—bow, and cringe, and tremble and quake—Fall down and worship over sovereign lord, the Mob!" Anyone who vocally defended the British connection risked life and limb. As Isaac Wilkins wrote to loyalist publisher James Rivington on May 13, 1775, before Wilkins departed New York City for England, "I leave America, and every endearing connection, because I will not raise my hand against my sovereign."

Prudent Loyalists kept their thoughts to themselves, especially after Continental commander Charles Lee arrived in February 1776, bringing with him a more warlike attitude toward the British and British sympathizers. Lee's troops were soon busy building fortifications against an expected British military incursion. George Washington arrived as well, more civil than his fellow Virginian but just as determined to defend American interests with force. Wisely, Tryon left the City for a safer haven on the British warship *Halifax*, and from his cabin there dissolved the colony's assembly. When Tryon applied to General William Howe, in Boston, for troops to prop up the royal government, Howe snidely replied that the entire British expeditionary force would soon descend on the City. Tryon did not share this news with the Loyalists or the increasingly hostile colonial militia massing in the City.

———

With Tryon's departure and John Lamb's volunteer artillery seizing the cannon from the battery for undetermined future use, the Loyalists could see that they had little chance to reverse the course of rebellion. Only the most intrepid or stubborn Loyalists refused to depart. When in July 1776 independence was declared, the Continental Congress drafted oaths of abjuration for those who remained in the City: "I, A. B., do solemnly swear that I do renounce, refuse, and abjure any allegiance or obedience to George III, the King of Great Britain, and that I will to the utmost of my power support, maintain, and defend the Independence of the United-States of America." For the Loyalists who had to swallow this bitter pill, the British could not come soon enough.

Meanwhile, Lee's two regiments in the City were joined by an estimated 10,000 Continentals, and by July the number grew to over 15,000. To these men, distributed among the hastily constructed fortifications on Long Island, Lower Manhattan, and both sides of the Hudson, would fall the fate of the Revolution, or so everyone believed. Washington feared that should the British take the City, they could move up the Hudson and prevent communication between the northern and southern colonies. Here he would make his stand.

It was clear to Washington and his officers in New York City that the inalienable rights that the Continental Congress proclaimed in the Declaration of Independence had to be won on the battlefield. New York City was an obvious objective given Whitehall's decision to commit British forces to a full-scale effort. Its central location and the size of its Loyalist contingent made the decision a natural one. On June 22, 1776, British forces numbering 40,000 soldiers, marines, and naval personnel appeared off Staten Island, an armada of over 100 warships and troop ships whose masts appeared to one Patriot observer as "thick as a forest." Henry Knox, one of Washington's commanders, wrote his wife on the eve of the battle, "The eyes of all America are upon us,—the matters which we are to act are of infinitely high import as we play our part posterity will bless or curse us."

A yearlong virtual siege of royal troops in Boston, featuring the ravages of a smallpox epidemic and the crippling battles of Concord and Bunker Hill, had not convinced Prime Minister Lord North's government or military planners in Whitehall that a war was unwinnable. Instead, they planned an ambitious two-pronged attack on the Patriots. A numerous force of Royal Navy and army personnel would drive the Continental Army from New York City. At the same time generous peace terms would be offered to both Washington and a delegation from the Congress.

On August 22, General Howe and his brother Admiral Richard Howe struck. Pitched battles on Long Island routed Continental units. As Pennsylvania Lieutenant Colonel Daniel Brodhead later recalled of the fighting around Flatbush, in what is now the borough of Brooklyn, the Continentals tried to "make a stand, but [other troops] . . . running thro' our files broke them, and in the confusion many of our men run with them. I did all in my power to rally the musquetry & Riflemen, but to no purpose." British delay, help from a stormy weather system, and the courage of his officers allowed Washington to manage a series of retreats and save the bulk of his forces from encirclement and destruction, but at the end of the day, all but the island of Manhattan lay in the hands of the Howe brothers' men. As Washington reported to Congress on September 2, 1776, "Our situation is truly distressing. The Check our Detachment sustained on the 27th. Ulto [last] has dispirited too great a proportion of our Troops and filled their minds with apprehension and dispair."

Captain Alexander Hamilton was in the thick of the fight, commanding a company of artillery and maneuvering his battery with a skill and courage remarkable for someone who had little experience of war. He managed to keep his company intact in the course of the retreat, and would serve with distinction when Washington's army resumed limited offensive activity in Trenton and Princeton, New Jersey, at the end of the year. Washington saw merit in Hamilton and in 1777 asked him to serve as an aide-de-camp, part of an intimate body of men Washington referred to as his "family." Though the two men would part over a petty slight in 1781, they were soon reunited and Hamilton remained Washington's trusted aide until the latter's death. For his own part, Hamilton privately admitted that he had never grown to like Washington but found the connection a useful stepstool to public advancement.

Watching the battle unfold was Aaron Burr, a twenty-two-year-old aide-de-camp to General Israel Putnam, Washington's second-in-command. Burr watched with alarm as Washington's formations were outflanked over and over again. Still, he recognized that the retreat from New York was a military necessity.

Burr's realism was won at great cost. If the child was father to the man, Burr's childhood—filled with promise and travail—forecast the course of his adult life. Born in 1756, he was surrounded by piety, books, ill health, and genteel poverty. His father, also named Aaron Burr, was one of the leading New Jersey puritan ministers. His mother, Esther, was the daughter of the reverend Jonathan Edwards of Northampton, Massachusetts, a foremost figure in the Great Awakening of evangelical piety and preaching. But both mother and father died before Burr was two years old. For a brief time he and his sister were cared for by a family friend, then both became part of the family of uncle Timothy Edwards's brood.

A child's personality may be formed by the fear of separation, and surely Burr's desire to excel, to prove his place in his new family, owed something to the loss of his parents. But loss can also breed a secretiveness and a restiveness. Burr's adult life featured both. He roared through the College of New Jersey, graduating at sixteen, and studied first for the ministry and then for the bar. Denied an officer's commission by George Washington, Burr nevertheless proved himself intrepid in the disastrous invasion of Canada in the winter of 1775–1776. Ill health ended his role as a soldier in 1777, and poorer than when he entered the service, Burr found his prospects uncertain.

––––––––

With the battle of Long Island lost, representatives of the Congress agreed to meet with Admiral Lord Richard Howe on September 11, at a mansion on Staten Island under British control. Howe had a limited brief from his masters to end the hostilities and return the colonies to British rule. The Continental Congress's delegation, Edward Rutledge from South Carolina, John Adams from Massachusetts, and Benjamin Franklin from Pennsylvania, explained that with independence already declared, it could not be rescinded. Franklin knew Howe from his time in England, when Howe had asked Franklin to help resolve the growing crisis. Franklin was courteous during the meeting. By contrast, Adams returned Howe's politeness with sharp disdain. Rutledge's contribution was a complaint about how oppressive royal government had been in his home colony—in effect, independence was imposed on South Carolina planters and merchants by British intransigence. Although Howe had agreed to treat the three men as representatives of Congress, rather than private citizens, and admitted that he would find the loss of the colonies like "the loss of a brother," he found their stance unacceptable. Rutledge reported back to Washington that everything now depended on the general's defense of the City. Egged on by Tryon, now "dancing attendance" on General William Howe at his headquarters, he and his brother Richard ordered the resumption of the attack on the island of Manhattan. Within a week it was theirs.

The retreating Continental Army left behind thousands of prisoners of war. The fate of those left behind was not enviable. Brodhead's son, an officer, was exchanged, but soon after the battle died of his wounds. Ordinary soldiers faced hellacious conditions. The British, suspicious of the humanitarian motives of "flag ships" sent by Patriot authorities carrying foodstuffs for the prisoners, prevented direct delivery and often simply diverted the victuals to their own tables. Confined in rotting hulks in the harbor or warehouses, jails, and other makeshift prisons on land, denied rations by corrupt civil and military officials, nearly one-third of the prisoners of war died.

The City's location and the some 30,000 British troops quartered there made it the center of British operations for the rest of the war. The military governor of the city was the commander in chief of the British Army in America. Under the laws of war as understood at the time, and perhaps more important, because the crown and its military commanders in America were still hoping for a negotiated settlement to the rebellion, New York City and Long Island were not treated as conquered territory. Its warehouses, churches, and public buildings were appropriated for the soldiers, but "quartering" of the army personnel in private dwellings was common in colonial times (though sometimes hotly resisted by colonists). Food, firewood, wagons, and horses were taken for the use of the army, with compensation. The usual complaints against the army's commissaries and other agents had a basis in fact, but soldiers living in barracks behaved better than soldiers living off the countryside as a rule.

Members of the civilian population were hired when necessary to perform domestic tasks, but no one was put to slave labor except those already enslaved. Although suspected Patriots were forced to flee or at least to conform to British orders, there was no reign of terror imposed like that in the ancient Roman or more recent English and Irish civil wars. The British commanders regarded themselves as gentlemen, sometimes living sumptuously to the disgust of civilians, but none acted the role of a Nero. Not even the most vicious Patriot wag accused General Howe of setting fire to his own city, though burn it did shortly after Washington departed.

For these and other reasons, the Loyalists in the City and those who had journeyed to it to escape Patriot harassment in the surrounding countryside expected to fare far better than the defeated Patriots. Joyous at the arrival of British arms and the disgraceful rout of Washington's army, they flooded into the streets, donned florets in their caps, and swore their undying affection for the king. Long muzzled by real or imagined threats of violence, supporters of the crown hoped that better days were ahead. Exiled Loyalists returned to join those who had to keep a low profile during the fighting. Some among them volunteered for military service against their former neighbors, and City regiments of Loyalists sailed with British regulars to occupy Savannah, Georgia; Charles Town, South Carolina; and even more distant points. Meanwhile, in the City, former political leaders like the DeLanceys expected to find that the occupying forces were willing to restore civilian control to the City, making it in effect the second capital of a revived empire. They were sorely disappointed. British commanders imposed martial law. In vain, the Loyalist leadership presented a petition to General Howe, military governor of the City, asking for the return of civilian self-government. But New York City was a British armed camp, and Loyalists found their homes and property sequestered to the British war effort. Supporters of the Revolution fared markedly worse. Their belated protestations of loyalty were invariably suspect. Exile and confiscation of their property for use by the British forces followed.

Still, families split by the occupation continued to visit with one another. Ties of kinship often outweighed boundaries that military exigency imposed. Men and women of prominent Patriot and Loyalist families crossed the lines to visit with relatives, with the open or at least tacit approval of authorities. Passes were issued by both sides, complained of by both sides, and availed of by both sides. The laxity of enforcement did not lessen the pains of separation or the dislocation of established ties, especially when relatives were on opposite sides of the political fence.

So, too, the business community on both sides of the struggle found ways to circumvent the edicts of military authorities. After all, the very reason for New York City's prominence was its position as a port for export and import of durable goods, agricultural products, and human chattel. In prior years, a good portion of these were smuggled in from or smuggled out to French, Dutch, and Spanish markets in violation of the Navigation Acts. Evading the law against trading with the enemy in time of war, during the periodic wars for empire from 1703 to 1763, the City's merchants covertly imported French molasses, Spanish wines, and Dutch tea. In fact, the City's business community had been the slowest and most reluctant section of the population to embrace nonimportation and other forms of economic protest against Parliament in 1772 and after. During the Revolutionary War, enterprising businessmen had to be even slyer than before the war, for the penalties for illicit trade were far harsher during the War for Independence than during the wars for empire. Still, Loyalist merchants in the City bought and sold agricultural goods from Patriot farmers and sold imported goods to Patriot shopkeepers in New Jersey, Connecticut, and across the Hudson River in Patriot-occupied New York. The profits outweighed the risks, and the trade simply continued through prewar networks. Revolutionary state legislatures passed increasingly stern warnings against trading with the enemy, governors pressed locals for compliance, and the British authorities cracked down on some merchants, but the trafficking continued.

One group of people actually fared better in the occupied City than they had before the war. At least one-tenth of New York City's population before the occupation lived in slavery. Slaves worked at the docks, as porters, street cleaners, in craft shops, and as domestics. The City had seen two major slave uprisings, in 1712 and 1741. Despite the fears these revolts evoked, slaves in the city enjoyed more personal autonomy than slaves on plantations to the south, having more time to themselves, often earning pocket money, and finding ways to gather together away from the prying eyes of masters, bosses, and the authorities.

Retreating Revolutionaries had taken their slaves with them, sometimes sending trusted slaves to slip back into the City to carry away property. The war brought greater mobility to these slaves, sometimes allowing them to act on their own initiative. The most striking example of the latter was slaves freeing themselves by crossing the lines into the City. The British encouraged this activity, offering freedom to Patriots' slaves who left their masters. Although formal freedom only was offered to male slaves, bondsmen brought their families with them. Revolutionary authorities were largely powerless to prevent the black flight to freedom, for all the methods by which slave colonies prevented slave mobility—patrols, informants, and severe punishment of those recaptured—did not work in this situation. What is more, the state governments of New York, New Jersey, and Connecticut did not offer freedom to slaves who deserted their Loyalist masters. By war's end, there were 3,000 former slaves in the City, joining the free black population that had never left.

Former slaves in the British-occupied city bettered themselves, but they suffered the same want as their poor white counterparts. Food and firewood were always in short supply. Those who had hard currency could buy foodstuffs from neighboring farms (sometime owned and operated by Patriots), but the City was overstuffed with civilian refugees. Loyalist civilians had to compete with better-funded British newcomers for necessities. Every civilian except those at the top of society had to compete with the buying power of the British commissary general and the British officers. A city whose warehouses were once stuffed to overflowing with flour and beef was suffering pervasive and nagging hunger.

Information about the course of the war was heard very differently in the Loyalist and secret Patriot camps in the City. Word of the surrender of Cornwallis's southern army after the siege of Yorktown, in September 1781, was quietly cheered among the Patriots and greeted with muted concern in Loyalist quarters. News followed that Lord North's government in England had fallen, and the Shelburne Whigs, now in charge, were negotiating a peace with the United States, France, and Spain. At the end of 1782 New York City was still occupied by British troops when authorities on both sides learned that a draft treaty had been signed by the peacemakers in Paris. The Loyalists were dispirited. British Commander Sir Henry Clinton, based in the City, lamented "never was despair or distraction more strongly painted than in the countenance I momentarily see. And I do declare that I am often obliged to retire to my room to avoid hearing dispersions too justly founded." Some Loyalists even papered the walls of public places with furious denunciations of the crown for agreeing to a peace. Other Loyalists, including remaining ministers of the Church of England, wrote the crown of their continued loyalty. They hoped that the crown would not "withdraw your royal protection from us." But the charred steeple of once-proud Trinity Church, the damage of the fire of 1776 never fully repaired, reminded the clergymen of what was now forever lost—an established Church of England. Clinton's replacement, Sir Guy Carleton, sent their piteous declaration to England in December 1782.

———

In the final years of the war, Loyalists in New York City were directly affected by events in the surrounding countryside. During the war Loyalists survived in the no-man's land of shifting loyalties and guerrilla actions contiguous to the City. From the end of 1781 through the end of 1783, Loyalist militia from the surrounding areas retired to the City, by then the last stronghold of British power in the north. Royal forces that occupied Savannah and Charles Town also began arriving in the summer of 1782 and continued to pour in through the winter of 1783. With them came more Loyalists. The terms of the peace arrived at the same time and dashed hopes of compensation for lost property and restoration of former status. Some Loyalists left the new nation. The DeLanceys decamped to England and in exile lamented to Parliament that the sums allotted to the Loyalists in England were "not equal to one third of the amount" of claims of property confiscated. Rich in New York City, they became pastoralists or professional soldiers in the home country. Members of the younger generation would in time return to New York. Some Loyalists already in exile, like old and infirm Peter Van Schaack, only wanted to return. As he wrote to John Jay, "My heart warms whenever our country (I must call it my country) is the subject, and in my separation from it, I have dragged at each remove a lengthening chain." Two years later Van Schaack arrived in New York City and Jay was there to greet him.

In the meantime, Carleton, pressed into staying on in New York City by Lord North, found himself acting as a diplomat (negotiating with Governors Clinton, John Hancock of Massachusetts, and William Livingston, who removed himself to New Jersey in 1770 and replaced Franklin's son William as governor in 1776), a banker, a civil magistrate, a disbursement officer, a relocation specialist, and a host to the relatives of American Generals and revolutionary politicians. Carleton was an experienced administrator and soldier, serving in Canada and the colonies. Unlike other British commanders, he honored the promise of freedom to the slaves who fled Patriot owners before the signing of the draft treaty. To do otherwise would have been, in his mind, "a dishonorable violation of the public faith." Although he graciously made every attempt "within my situation" to perform all of these tasks as he related to Hancock on April 11, 1783, a month later he told another correspondent, Governor William Browne of Bermuda, that he could do little "until the present heats have cooled."

Those heats still burned in the countryside, as suspected Loyalists like John Cook reported on September 16, 1783. The treaty of peace had not yet been ratified, and the Duchess County committee was not in a forgiving mood. "The language of the committees is that none shall rule but the majority of the people, and that the com-

{ *Chapter One* }

mittees represent the majority, that the acts and agreements of the Congress, the legislatures, governors and rulers, are all to be subject to the will of the people expressed by the committees." Abuse, dispossession, and the threat of death fell upon every suspected Loyalist in the areas around the City.

Although some in Britain, including King George III, wanted the treaty of peace to include a provision for return of Loyalists' confiscated property outside the City, that was not possible. The property had been sold at auction by the state government to finance its part in the war effort. The only real assurance the crown offered was relocation to Canada, the Caribbean, and the home islands. The only compensation the treaty required was to Patriots who could document that their slaves had left with the British forces.

While the revolutionary armies dispersed and the revolutionary leaders consolidated their hold on state and local government, Loyalists continued to depart. Over 60,000 joined their former neighbors in England, Nova Scotia, and Canada and petitioned Parliament for monetary settlements. Other Loyalists threw themselves on the mercy of their former enemies. They turned to friends and family for succor in this endeavor, as well as soliciting the support of Carleton. On August 1, 1783, he reported his concern for "a number of gentlemen, clergy and merchants now resident in this city and neighborhood, who from their attachment to Government and connection with the army, deem it unsafe to remain here after the king's Troops remove from hence." When alarming news of new legislation aimed at Loyalists who did remain reached the City on April 21, they petitioned Carleton, "fearful of future suits from rules of New York State . . . for rents or supposed trespasses." Carleton knew that in 1778 Henry Clinton had ordered occupiers of abandoned buildings to pay rent for the use of the poor, but what was to be done with these wartime occupants now that the British were departing? One answer came in a general order of June 16, 1783: "All such estates were to be immediately delivered up to their proprietors or to their attornies."

In the waning days of spring 1783, Loyalist newspapers began to find virtue in Washington and other revolutionary leaders who had only the year before been targets of abuse. This was one more bit of evidence, if such was needed, of the ambiguous and often shifting allegiance of men within the City. William Smith Jr., whose ties to the Livingston clan had gained him sanctuary for a time on their Hudson River estates, was back in the City and recorded the efforts of his Loyalist friends to reincorporate themselves into the civic life of the new state.

More important in a way was the effort of Loyalist merchants to establish their new attachment to the republican system. They argued that their presence was a boon to the City and the state's economy. They knew that the broken tie of empire would end the special privileges they had enjoyed in British home markets and the lucrative West Indian trade, but they hoped they could still use their contacts to gain favorable credit and price terms from English suppliers. What is more, they knew that the war had dammed up but not diminished the demand for English and European durable goods in America. Before the final crisis that demand had fueled a "consumer revolution," a buying spree that filled colonial homes with porcelain table ware, silver tea and coffee services, upholstered furniture, and other luxury items. Their insight was prescient; orders for more of the same were already going out to British manufacturers.

November 21, 1783, was the beginning of four days' final debarkation of British troops. On November 25, New York's governor George Clinton and General Washington met at Tarrytown, on the Hudson, and rode together down to Harlem Heights to await word of the last British longboat ferrying His Majesty's troops to the ships in the East River. The two men tarried at a tavern, the city's taverns once again assuming pride of place for revolutionary gatherings. Another tavern, Fraunces, hosted Washington's December 4 farewell to his officers. His short talk was as courteous and formal as the man: "With a heart full of love and gratitude I now take leave of you. I most devoutly wish that your latter days may be as prosperous and happy as your former ones have been glorious and honorable." A final glass and he was away to resign his commission to the Congress, meeting at Annapolis, Maryland. His war was over.

Peace brought a reverse flow of former Revolutionaries into the City, seeking out personal possessions and reoccupying structures. In the final months of their occupation of the City, the British allowed this in-migration, though it was soon almost out of hand. The result was a city that looked somewhat like the prewar community. State authorities did not follow the British lead, however, instead preferring to legislate a continuation of the contest. For they knew, and Loyalists reading the treaty of peace soon learned, that it did not guarantee them a return of property outside of the City, or protect the property they occupied inside the City during the conflict. Worse still, it did not mandate the restoration of their citizenship.

But they had friends. Alexander Hamilton, returned from service as Washington's aide-de-camp, entered the City before the British departed to look after the affairs of his wife, Elizabeth Schuyler. He reported back to correspondents that many useful Loyalists— merchants, bankers, professionals—were departing the City because they feared peace would bring them a permanent subordinate status. Something should be done, he concluded, if the city was to reclaim its place in the commerce of the Atlantic World. To that end, he began the study of law, remarking to a friend, "I am learning how to fleece my neighbors." For his neighbors had passed laws that seemed to confirm the former Loyalists' worst fears. Their plight became the foundation of his law practice.

CHAPTER TWO

Laws and Lawyers for a Revolutionary Republic

Before the onset of hostilities, New York City was the capital of the colony. Dominated by moderate Whigs and Loyalists, the colonial assembly had refused to send representatives to the Second Continental Congress. More insistent was the Committee of Sixty, and on April 20, 1775, it named a slate of delegates to the Congress. The committee's authority for this act could not be the colonial charter, for the assembly still existed. So the committee reconstituted itself a provincial congress, and proceeded to act as if it represented the people. In this fashion, more for practical than theoretical or ideological reasons, the new government had to rest itself upon the ultimate sovereignty of the people rather than the crown. Henceforth, all revolutionary and subsequent republican self-government in the state would rest upon this foundation. When General Howe tried to reconstitute the colonial assembly the next year, he found it untrustworthy, dissolved it, and it never met again. Before 1777, the only legislative body for New York was the provincial congress.

Service in the new state's legislative body was taxing and could be perilous. The legislators fled the city as the British approached. The first session, meeting in White Plains on the Hudson, was abandoned for lack of a quorum. When enough members finally arrived, on July 9, 1776, the state declared its independence. A year passed before the delegates had a constitution. In the meantime, there was no executive and no judicial branch—giving the assembly something of the character of a debating society. The state constitution of 1777 filled the gaps, adopting the plan of checks and balances that John Adams had proposed for Massachusetts's constitution a year earlier. Voting for members was limited to freeholders, the older British idea that government should be chosen by those with "a stake" in society. Had the constitution been written in New York City, under the eyes of its radical street politicians like Isaac Sears, John Lamb, and Alexander McDougall; that is, had the British not occupied the city, it might have been a far more democratic document.

It is noteworthy that Article 35 of the constitution of the state provided that

> such parts of the common law of England, and of the statute law of England and Great Britain, and of the acts of the legislature of the colony of New York, as together did form the law of the said colony on the 19th day of April, in the year of our Lord one thousand seven hundred and seventy-five, shall be and continue the law of this State, subject to such alterations and provisions as the legislature of this State shall, from time to time, make concerning the same.

This essay is hardly the place to introduce to a reader the entire complexity of Anglo-American law or constitutionalism. Suffice it to relate that the "reception" of such portion of the common law already practiced in the colony was both a substantive and a procedural commitment. Patriot lawyers, including those who passed the bar in the waning years of conflict, studied the "forms of action," the grounds for which a person could bring a suit, the "writ" system of pleading by which cases were categorized and argued before a jury, and the case law or precedent system, by which prior cases on the same point determined the outcome of later cases. New York was not the only state to receive or incorporate the common law; in the wake of independence most of the new states did the same by statute. But equally important was the fact that the new republican government of the state had supplanted portions of the common law with legislative acts. The very basis by which common law was received in the constitution rested upon the act of a sovereign people, not on the authority of the king's courts or Parliament. New York's lawyers had to pay as much attention to this growing body of statutory law, including the Loyalist Code, as they did to older, less politically charged common-law concepts. Indeed, the body of law the legislature directed to Loyalists, hereafter called the Loyalist Code, itself was a departure from the very foundations of common law, for these men and women were being ostracized and penalized for their adherence to the English source of common law, the crown.

Still, according to Article 35, property held according to the common law and litigation commenced under common law would not be disrupted. No more obvious proof of the framers' disinclination to radicalize law could be found. The state constitution established a Council of Revision consisting of the judges of the supreme court, the governor, and the chancellor to examine all bills before they were passed in final form—one final safeguard against too radical a revision of the laws by a temporary majority of the legislature. The council made plain its intent to actively supervise the legislature, lest it innovate in too thorough a fashion. The legislature could override the recommendation of the council, however.

Under the terms of the new constitution, George Clinton of Ulster County was elected the first governor. He was an energetic and able politician, by his friends acquitted a "man of the people." Moreover, he had served in the Continental Army before his election, an asset because the fate of the state still hung in the balance of arms. No one knew better than he the danger that British forces presented to the new state. In the same month of September 1777 that the new government met under the constitution, General John Burgoyne and his troops marched south from Canada into the heartland of the state. The legislators kept their bags packed—military necessity dictated shifting their sessions from Fishkill to Kingston, then to Poughkeepsie, and finally to Albany. Fortunately for the Patriots, Burgoyne was defeated in a series of battles around the village of Saratoga and General Nicholas Herkimer's forces stopped a British thrust into the Finger Lakes Country. Although armed conflict in the state continued with Continental Army raids in force the next year against those Iroquois who had aided the British, and smaller raids enmeshing state militia and loyalist levies in combat, the new government was safe.

In 1777, when the possibility still existed that the British would either sever the state along the Champlain-Hudson line or at least win back a portion of the upstate, the authors of the new state constitution made conciliatory gestures to regain the loyalty of fence-sitters. The 13th Article promised "that no member of this State shall be disfranchised, or deprived of any the rights or privileges secured to the subjects of this State by this constitution, unless by the law of the land, or the judgment of his peers." In other words, due process of law was a hallmark of the new constitution, as it had been of the Magna Charta of England, over 500 years earlier.

In 1778, with the military threat receding, the majority in the legislature embarked on a campaign of harassing suspected Loyalists "by the law of the land." Although the invidious statutes began to appear soon after the state government was constituted, the approaching peace introduced a harsher tone in the enactments. By the end of the war, the statutes concerning the Loyalists ran to over 150 printed pages, a detailed code that applied only to those who would not renounce their old loyalty to home country and crown. The portion of this code that dealt with Loyalists in arms was comparatively small. The vast majority of the provisions dealt with taxes, debt, ownership of land and chattels, and other fiscal and property questions. The major concern of the legislature was not loyalism as a crime, but loyalism as a kind of civil disobedience for which the proper response was confiscation of personal estates, protection of Patriots against Loyalist legal actions, and imposition of rules barring certain kinds of defense motions by Loyalists.

Revolutionary lawyers in the legislature were writing the laws with one eye on the coming peace. All these provisions anticipated the time when the war would be over and former Loyalists would wager their law in the state's courts. Then the state courts would surely be overflowing with suits growing out of the Loyalist Code that former Loyalists, aided by counsel (some of whom would be Patriots), would contest. In other words, the authors of the statutes assumed that peace would bring resumption of the regular legal process.

Given this, a very important feature of the code can be teased out of its immensely detailed and overlapping provisions. Despite the carnage and animosity of the war, the revolutionary authors of the statutes believed in a rule of law. Civil war did not set aside law or the process of legislation. It might bend that process to favor the Patriot side; indeed its language betrayed the anger that many of the Patriot leaders in the legislature directed toward individual Loyalists, in particular those who took up arms to defend the crown, but it did not engage in the sort of sweeping lawlessness that characterized the conduct of victors at the end of other civil wars. The Loyalists lost their citizenship, but unlike runaway slaves or Native Americans, both of whom were treated far more harshly in New York than the Loyalists, those who refused to renounce their allegiance to king and empire did not lose their legal identity. They could still be sued and for the most part they could still defend themselves against suits. To repeat: in its treatment of the wartime enemy, the Loyalist Code confirmed that the foundation of republican state making was due process of law.

This said, the Loyalist Code took a very dim view indeed of those who would not join in the revolutionary cause. An Act of Banishment of 1778 began the campaign of legal harassment of Loyalists. Its preamble condemned slackers' "poverty of spirit" and "undue attachment to property." They had no place among a revolutionary people at war. The legislators lashed out at those who "ungratefully and insidiously" employed "a subtle dissemination of doctrines, fears and apprehensions" to sway "weak minded persons" from performing their revolutionary duty. With a preamble breathing such passion, the enacting portions of the statute could hardly have surprised any Loyalist. The oath of loyalty to the sovereign state was modeled, like the definition of treason, on older English oaths of allegiance to the crown and its succession. Failure to take the oath was punishable by banishment, forfeiture of all title to lands within the state and "hereafter" double taxes on all lands liable to state taxes.

The act of October 22, 1779, elaborated on the forfeiture of estates of suspected Loyalists. In form it was a general "bill of attainder," a civil or criminal imposition brought by the legislature instead of a court, in which the sufferers had no legal recourse or chance to defend themselves or present evidence. (The federal Constitution would explicitly bar states from passing such acts.) While the act accused the crown of being the real culprit, the crown was safe from prosecution. Instead, the losers were the Loyalists named in the act. "Attainted" were leading Loyalists like Oliver DeLancey, former speaker of the colonial assembly; Hudson River manor lords like Frederick Philipse; former councilors, mayors, merchants, substantial farmers, and just about everyone else of note who had not signed the oath of allegiance. All of the attainted were banished and if found within the state were to be adjudged guilty of felony and sentenced to death. For these men, there was no provision for due process, jury trial, or any of the other procedural guarantees that the Whigs had demanded from the crown during the crisis of the 1760s.

In what reads like an afterthought, perhaps a concession to those Patriots who thought the attainder had gone too far, the statute empowered grand juries to add to the list of names in the act other individuals whose property was confiscated and who could be seized. For these individuals, however, due process did apply. If such persons were indicted and summoned, failure to appear was a confession of guilt for which punishment would follow. Appearing, the suspect was entitled to a trial at law before a jury of the vicinage. In a further irony, the evidence of treason against the state was the same as evidence against those accused of treason in England, but unlike the English law, a full pardon was available to any person who took the oath of loyalty to the state—the harshness and pitilessness of the statute being an inducement for anyone caught in its net to shift his allegiance from crown to the sovereign state of New York.

The act then described the procedures for the confiscation of Loyalist estates. It did not mandate the sale of those estates, in effect holding them as hostage for Loyalists' shift of allegiance. This public escrow account would exist until 1781, when the sales began to private buyers. In the meantime, the legislature protected the economic interests of Patriot landowners by requiring those who occupied loyalist leaseholds to pay rent under the terms of the prewar leases.

The Seditious Libel Act of 1781 applied to anyone who took the oath but then in "preaching, teaching, speaking, or writing" any defense of the crown, or advising another that the crown might have any claim on that person's allegiance, undermined attachment to the new state. Such actions or speech was made a felony. There was no freedom of speech in the state, not when it came to political opinions, although Revolutionaries protested that the crown encroached on the freedom of speech due every Englishman, no matter where he resided. At the discretion of the judge, the court could convert a death sentence for a convict to three years' service on a ship of the U.S. Navy. This merciful alternative to capital punishment resembled the unlawful seizure of sailors in ports by Royal Navy "press gangs" to fill the crews of warships, one of the prime causes of anti-British rioting among Patriot crowds. Judging by the Loyalist Code, the legislature either had a short memory of the grounds alleged for the rebellion or, in contrary fashion, saw the utility of these older forms of oppression.

Neutrals could not count on the protection afforded by legal practitioners, as a statute in 1779 suspended all lawyers suspected of Loyalist sympathies until they applied to the state supreme court for reinstatement. The sheriff of the county where they resided had to bring to the court affidavits of between eight and sixteen "persons of established reputation and known attachment to the freedom and independence of America" to attest to the petitioner's zealous friendship to the new state. The statute exempted all lawyers who had served in the Continental Army or as delegates to state government or the Continental Congress. In a way the procedure bore similarities to the old English form of trial called compurgation. In it, parties at issue brought to court a body of witnesses who swore to the truth of the party's allegations or defense. Once again, the startling conclusion of this portion of the Loyalist Code is that the revolutionary republican state not only incorporated older English common law forms, it borrowed from English law the very impositions on American rights that Patriots condemned in the crisis.

One might reply that in wartime every nation adopts harsh laws to deal with internal enemies. In a civil war, like that waged in New York between 1776 and 1783, one should not be surprised that the state legislature tried to protect its patriotic citizens' interests. Another of these aids was the Trespass Act of May 11, 1783. It provided that Patriots whose property "within the power of the enemy" was taken or occupied or destroyed by Loyalists could bring an action of trespass against the Loyalist. The act provided damages equivalent to back rent. If a Loyalist purchased or received any such property, or benefitted from occupation of it, the Loyalist was not allowed to plead that the British made him do it (military necessity), or that he did not know that he was taking property that belonged to a Patriot. If a Patriot destroyed Loyalist property, even illegally, no civil action would lie against the Patriot.

If the keystone of the Patriot legislative efforts to punish the Loyalists was the new Trespass Act, the idea of using the courts to collect back rent was nothing new. In the years before the war began, New York was roiled by a series of rent wars. These raged up and down the Hudson River. On the east side of the river, huge estates, some dating back to the Dutch "patroonships" and others of more recent establishment, hosted hundreds of leaseholds. The renters were family farmers, some of (Protestant) French Huguenot, Dutch, German, and Scots, but mostly English extraction. In 1750s and 1760s they raised less grain and more havoc in response to the manor lords' attempt to raise rents. Chief among the landlords were Frederick Philipse, Stephen Van Renssalaer, and Robert Livingston Jr., who divided among them thousands of acres and rented them out as a source of income. The settlers, by contrast, saw their parcels as homestead and farmstead, producing enough for their families, with the surplus going into the market. Which of these concepts was the more modern and capitalistic and which the more backward looking and traditional sets historians at odds, but for the contestants in the rent wars, concept bowed to action. The landlords tried to use the courts to enforce their will, and the renters used force to shut the courts down. The renters turned to the crown, petitioning for the king to intercede. In the process, rent itself became a point of contention. Did long usage trump written contracts? Was occupation at the will of the landlord or did a settler's improvement of the land convey a kind of title to it? James Duane, representing the landlords, won the legal contest; the protestors were ejected from their leaseholds, and rent joined liberty as a watchword of New York justice.

Thus the passage of the Trespass Act had a far longer, and much more complex, genesis than simple vengeance against the former Loyalists. Property held to rent was as sacred to the makers of New York law as property in Indian lands, property in Loyalist estates, and property in slaves. In all of the latter, New York law protected the property owner. But the act took these concepts into the Loyalist Code. Dispossessed of their property and driven from its premises by the British, Patriot owners could bring suit for damages in the amount of unpaid rent. The claimants were to determine the rent owed—no guidelines were given in the act. Defendants were not allowed to argue that they acted pursuant to "any military order or command whatsoever, for such occupancy, injury, destruction, purchase or receipt." Although the act was an ex post facto law, permitting a suit for damages for civil wrongs that were not wrong when they took place, the legislature regarded it as a "remedial" act. In any case, the state of New York was a sovereign and a victor, and thus could enact those laws it wished.

The Council of Revision created by the constitution, under its power of reviewing legislation, tried to stop the act from going into effect, but the legislature passed it over the council's stay and Clinton signed it. A year later, with Robert R. Livingston returned to the state as its chancellor and thus a member of the council, the council did prevent an Alien Act from being added to the Loyalist Code. Livingston himself saw merit in those "who wish to suppress all violences, to soften the rigour of the laws against the loyalists, and not to banish them from that social intercourse which may, by degrees, obliterate the remembrance of past misdeeds." The council condemned the proposed Alien Act for violating the treaty with Great Britain and the law of nations with the result that the legislature backed down.

Clinton sat on the council and had little use for the Loyalists. He supported a policy of scorched earth for them. "Damn the Tory rascals," he is reported to have said on more than one occasion. Clinton was not alone in this sentiment. When, after peace returned, former Loyalists left the city and traveled to their old haunts up the Hudson, they met violent handling. This the governor made little effort to oppose or punish.

Two obstacles stood in the way of the full deployment of the Loyalist Code after the Peace Treaty of 1783 was ratified at the beginning of 1784. The first was the strenuous efforts of Loyalists to conciliate their former opponents. In this they found allies in Clinton's party's aristocratic rivals, the Schuylers and the Livingstons. Philip Schuyler represented the old Dutch aristocracy and Clinton was, by comparison, an arriviste. The two men respected one another and had worked together in the early days of the protest but a breach was opened when Clinton defeated Schuyler in the first gubernatorial election. Clinton would hold the office until 1795, despite efforts by Schuyler and his allies to break Clinton's near stranglehold on the upstate vote.

Defeated at the polls, the Schuylers did not retreat from politics. The Schuyler daughters cemented new political alliances through marriage, one to up-and-coming lawyer Alexander Hamilton. The affiliation between the young Hamilton and his father-in-law was by all accounts one of genuine affection and mutual loyalty, unlike Hamilton's tumultuous relationship with Washington. The Schuyler-Clinton rivalry fed into a more lasting and more ideologically grounded estrangement of the conservative wing of the Whig party in the state from the Clinton majority in the legislature.

As the gap between the two sides widened, the Loyalist Code become a focal point of their disagreement. Led by men like Schuyler and Robert Livingston, and their younger associates John Jay and James Duane, conservatives opposed additions to the code, while the Clinton forces pressed for more anti-Loyalist legislation. When the peace came, the conservatives supported reconciliation with the former Loyalists. Jay called the Trespass Act's timing "destitute of even resemblance to reason." But the conservative Patriots could not stop its passage or its deployment. Indeed, John Jay's family sought damages under the act. They employed Aaron Burr to represent them in the Mayor's Court. After all, it was property and property rights that concerned them.

The second obstacle to full deployment of the code lay outside of Clinton and the New York state legislature's majority control. Among the problems of the period was the growing indebtedness of the confederation government. With requisitions from the states lagging and the value of the continental currency falling, the Congress had to find sources of income. One way to retire the debt was to grow the national economy, a project to which the commercial enterprise of the City of New York was essential. The former Loyalist merchants resident in the City were thus vital to the prospects of the confederation. For their part, the former Loyalists hoped that this commercial activity would enable them to work their way back into citizenship.

While the Congress had little direct authority over Clinton and his government, it did have authority over the diplomacy of the new nation. Congress sent delegates to Europe to negotiate the peace. While the treaty they helped frame did not guarantee the return of

Loyalist property, it did make a concession to former Loyalists who were owed money before the war by Patriots: "Article IV. It is agreed that creditors on either side shall meet with no legal impediment to recovery of the full value in sterling money of all bona fide debts heretofore contracted." Even more important was Article V: "It is agreed that Congress shall earnest recommend to the legislatures of the respective states to provide for the restitution of all estates, rights and properties, which have been confiscated, belonging to all real British subjects, and also of the estates rights and properties of all persons resident in districts in the possession of his Majesty's arms, and who have not born arms against the said United States."

The objects of the treaty's solicitude were British subjects, but some former Loyalists fit this category and some British subjects in 1783 hoped to become citizens of the new states after the terms of the treaty were ratified. Just as political loyalties during the war were flexible, so political identity after the war was fluid. There was no national citizenship in the new United States (that would not come until the Fourteenth Amendment to the Constitution, in 1868). One was a citizen of the United States if one was a citizen of a state. Thus, if former Loyalists or British subjects in the City wanted the benefits of citizenship, they must be secured from the state of New York. The Loyalist Code posed serious but not insurmountable difficulties for these men.

Members of the New York legislature knew the contents of the draft treaty when they began consideration of the Trespass Act. The draft treaty was circulated after November 30, 1782, and was accepted by Congress on April 15, 1783, though it did not bind the combatants until September 3, 1783, and only in January 1784 was it ratified by Congress, after which its provisions went into effect. The terms of the treaty, and the law of war by which the terms were to be interpreted, would become one avenue for the former Loyalists and likeminded British subjects in the City to begin their reincorporation or incorporation into the new state's polity.

But looming over the entire process of rapprochement between Britain and the United States, and therefore over the relations between former Loyalists and their estranged Patriot neighbors, was the debt question. As late as the end of February 1786, the British government informed Congress that the United States had not fulfilled its obligations under the treaty.

> The fourth Article of the same treaties as clearly stipulates, that Creditors on either side shall meet with no lawful impediment to the recovery of the full value in sterling money, of all bona fide debts heretofore contracted. The little attention paid to the fulfilling this engagement on the part of the Subjects of the United States in general, and the direct breach of it in many particular instances, have already reduced many of the King's Subjects to the utmost degree of difficulty and distress; nor have their applications for redress, to those whose situations in America naturally pointed them out as the guardians of publick faith, been as yet successful in obtaining them that justice to which, on every principle of law as well as of humanity, they were clearly and indisputably entitled.

The Trespass Act was one part of that problem. It had to be overcome, or at least constrained, before the debt problem could be redressed.

———

As the war ravaged the old landscape of deference politics and legal practice, it opened fertile ground for a new generation of American lawyers. Gone from the bar and bench were Loyalist attorneys and judges. Resulting vacancies provided opportunities for newly minted lawyers to find clients, including former Loyalists. It also improved the business of older lawyers who had chosen sides correctly. On new and existing members of the bar the establishment of the confederation and the new state governments imposed public responsibilities. As Egbert Benson, in the midst of drafting legislation about the Loyalists, wrote to Robert R. Livingston, "the preservation of the country" depended on the lawyers' continuing commitment to public service. Livingston, busy at Congress, hardly needed Benson's encouragement to keep a shoulder to the public weal. Men like Benson and Livingston did not give up their private practices, however. (The state legislature finally decided, in 1792, when Aaron Burr was attorney general, that the state's legal officials "should not act, in any private suit, unless the people of this state shall be interested.")

Peace brought more opportunity for work and imposed more work on lawyers. Embroiled in the political wars of the postwar era, obligated to serve in public posts, burdened with private practice, the revolutionary lawyer worked harder and had more responsibility than his colonial counterpart. Some must have shared the sentiments expressed by Archibald Maclaine, a North Carolina revolutionary lawyer, when he wrote in 1783, "how much I wish for a quiet retreat from the busy world."

No one was more avid to enter that busy world than Alexander Hamilton. No one was better fit by his exertions during the war to represent the revolutionary generation and the prospects of the new nation than he. Eager for advancement in both the political and the professional arenas, Hamilton found himself in the very center of the postwar Loyalist controversy in New York City. At twenty-six years of age, "slight and thin shouldered, with a distinctly Scottish appearance, with a florid complexion, reddish brown hair, and sparkling blue eyes," he was an attractive addition to the dinner table and a loyal friend. "Touchy" and sometimes violently combative, "he never outgrew the stigma of his illegitimacy" but he was much loved by his friends.

After he left Washington's side, Hamilton's real capital was almost nonexistent, but his social capital, his circle of friends and former associates, was sizable. On this he built less with cynical calculation than with genuine attachment. The first and perhaps most important of these attachments was marriage to Elizabeth Schuyler in the late fall of December 1780. The marriage's benefits to him far exceeded the value of the Schuyler family connection. Her loyalty and strength was always there for him, even when he strayed.

Unlike almost all of his comrades who entered the legal profession in the waning years of the war, Hamilton did not "read" law in the office of a member of the bar. Such preparation was onerous and much complained of at the time, for the apprentice counselor spent most of his time drafting legal documents. Instead, Hamilton studied law on his own and then compiled a 177-page manual, which he entitled "Practical Proceedings in the Supreme court of the state of New York." Although the original has disappeared, it was copied and passed down hand to hand by lawyers who followed him to the bar.

The text was typical of the man, picaresque and pedantic by turns. He wrote it for his own use: if A, then you do this, if B, then you do that. As dry as common law procedure was, the manual was nevertheless not. Hamilton transformed gray old writ pleading into a lively step-by-step helper to the uninitiated, a veritable "Idiot's Guide" to New York procedure.

He added his own thinking to the manual, as if he were a teacher of procedure instead of its student. He sprinkled "There seems to be no reason for this" and "I see no reason why" throughout the text. He inserted short essays within the categories on why some ancient forms of pleading were no longer used and no longer necessary, for example as "some of a more liberal cast begin to have some faint idea that the end of suits at law is to investigate the merits of the cause, not to entangle you in the nets of technical terms."

A voracious reader from childhood, while studying for the bar Hamilton consumed the classics of common law, natural law, and the law of nations. For the latter field especially it was a heady time. In 1760, the Swiss philosopher and diplomat Emmerich de Vattel's *Law of Nations According to Scientific Principles* had just been translated into English. In 1775, Benjamin Franklin thanked a Dutch correspondent for providing three copies of the book. "I am much obliged by the kind present you have made us of your edition of Vattel. It came to us in good season, when the circumstances of a rising state make it necessary frequently to consult the law of nations." He provided a copy to members of Congress, where, Franklin said, it was widely consulted. Sometime between the summer of 1782 and the winter of 1784, Hamilton must have found and pored over a copy of Vattel, with results that are traced below.

In July 1782, a mere three months after beginning his self-tutorial, Hamilton applied for the bar and was admitted to practice by the New York Supreme Court. As an officer serving in the Continental Army, he did not have to clerk for the three years required of civilians. The supreme court records showed that he first appeared for a client the following October. He then moved from Albany to New York City and rented an office. Hamilton was never still for long. He would travel up the Hudson to serve in the state legislature in Albany, then to Philadelphia to represent New York in Congress, back to

Albany, where the state supreme court sat, then again to home and family in the City sometimes with Betsy in tow. The revolutionary generation of lawyer politicians was ambulatory, some like Adams, Jay, and Jefferson crossing the Atlantic, others like Hamilton and Burr moving up and down the rivers and along the coastline of the new nation.

Hamilton was not as thrifty as others who traveled in the new nation's politics. He spent freely on clothing, lodging, and dining. For this and his family he needed a source of revenue, and the law did not fully provide for his needs. Never as wealthy as his higher-status friends, Hamilton joined in speculative projects like the Bank of New York and helped put together various land development deals. Bold and daring in his finances, like a gambler on a roll, Hamilton lived on the edge of wealth next to the precipice of poverty.

His various financial schemes did not adversely affect his law practice. For example, Hamilton found himself involved in the biggest land dispute of the day—the battle over the Livingston Manor— soon after he passed the bar. In 1783, Robert R. Livingston was the heir to the Clermont estate and found himself at legal odds with Zacharias Hoffman over some 500 acres of woodland, 500 acres of meadow, and various barns, milldams, and other structures. Livingston claimed that Hoffman was trespassing and hired Morgan Lewis, a young attorney, to file suit against Hoffman in the state supreme court. Such acts not only attached the financial interest of the new generation of lawyers to the great families, they created lasting webs of patronage and clientage.

Hoffman replied that he had leased the land and had the paperwork to prove it. On that basis Hoffman had occupied the land for over twenty years. Egbert Benson, and later, Hamilton appeared for the defendant. Hamilton's role was muted, for his political future required the amity of the plaintiff. Still, cases like this did not hurt his credibility, and the fact that he took part in it demonstrated his growing reputation. Hamilton would later shine in arguing for a new trial on a writ of error when Hoffman lost the case. A bystander at the appeal later recalled that Hamilton spoke for two hours, earnestly and with great "emphasis" to convince the court that a jury verdict might be overturned. He lost, but his reputation was burnished by the effort.

Reputation did not pay the bills, however, any more than eloquently argued losing causes. Fortunately, Hamilton found a ready source of income in admiralty cases. He served as a "proctor" or legal counsel in suits brought by men who had invested in privateering ventures and sought a return on their investment when ships and cargoes captured by privateers were brought into the port of New York. Investors who had put money into these ventures vied for their portion of these seizures. Cases of this sort were time consuming but brought in a steady income.

Hamilton knew that British merchants who did business in New York and former Loyalists who faced legal retaliation under the Trespass Act needed representation. Joshua Waddington belonged in the former category. The British merchants whom Joshua served were not Loyalists per se, but they intended to remain in the state and faced a crippling demand for back rent for occupation of the Rutgers family brewhouse if the provisions of the Trespass Act stood unopposed. This was not a test case in the modern sense of the word—a case brought to establish a basic right. But it soon became a case that everyone in the legal community, especially the Loyalist community, watched closely. If Rutgers's claim was established in full, the Loyalists of the city would be impoverished. If the Mayor's Court bench denied some part of the claim, or all of it, the Loyalists would be able to resume their commercial endeavors safer from harassment. Peeking out from the background of the suit was a potent and divisive issue—a separation of powers dispute. Were courts independent branches of government, co-equal with legislative and executive branches? Or were courts weaker branches of government, in some sense agencies of the executive and legislative bodies? If a single court, indeed a court at the bottom of the judicial totem pole, could strike down a portion, or the entirety, of an act of the legislature, did that not make the courts equal partners in republican self-government? This notion, codified and explored under the rubric of "checks and balances" was not a part of Hamilton's brief, but it would become a part of his defense of federal constitutionalism in later years.

Joining Hamilton in this (as in other cases) was young Henry Brockholst Livingston. They had met at Elizabethtown when Hamilton was on leave from the army and they became fast friends. Livingston was the son of William Livingston (the first elected governor of the state of New Jersey and brother of Robert R. Livingston). The Livingston family secured its place in the next generation of the aristocracy of the state by marrying into the old Dutch patroon Van Cortland and Van Rensselaer families and co-opting up-and-coming men like George Clinton. One of the Livingston daughters, Maria, married James Duane when late in life he decided to abandon bachelorhood. Brockholst, as he was later called, was aide-de-camp to General Philip Schuyler, thus an ally by marriage as well as conservative leanings of Hamilton. He was admitted to practice in New York in 1783, a year after Hamilton and often joined him in representing clients; thus his career path was similar, although his ancestry and Hamilton's could not have been farther apart. Later in life he would accept an invitation from President Thomas Jefferson to join the U.S. Supreme Court, and the Senate speedily confirmed his nomination.

If Hamilton had a rival at the bar from his generation, it was another of Brockholst Livingston's intimates, Aaron Burr. Indeed, Hamilton, Burr, Edward Livingston, and James Kent would study together for the bar in Albany. Burr ran his health ragged preparing for the bar exam in Albany, New York, but he passed with flying colors and was admitted to the bar in 1782. A successful practice of law required sponsors, for sponsors brought rich clients, and both demanded that Burr pay court to powerful families like the Morrises and the Schuylers. Burr also made friends with leading lawyers like William Livingston and Melancton Smith. Asking the powerful for favors meant obligating oneself to perform favors, and Burr was good as his word.

All of these men would go on to high public office. Burr would serve in the U.S. Senate and as vice president of the country. Livingston would end up in New Orleans and write its legal code when it entered the United States as part of the Louisiana Purchase. Kent would read law in Egbert Benson's office and begin practice in 1785. Later he would serve as a member of the state supreme court and then as its chancellor. His commentaries on the law would rival those of Joseph Story.

Young Burr stayed in the City after passing the bar, and handled over sixty cases in the Mayor's Court. Eighteen of these rested on the Trespass Act, with Burr representing Patriots seeking back rent. Burr's office on Wall Street was close to the Mayor's Court courtroom in City Hall and his home was on Maiden Lane, within eyeshot of the brewhouse site. Burr was in attendance when the court opened its 1784 session on February 24, representing Daniel Tiere, administrator of the estate of John Henry Tiere, against Adam Fink, Peter Merry, and David Ruyter. Two weeks earlier Sheriff Marinus Willet had served papers for Burr on Fink and Merry. Ruyter was "non est," having departed along with other British merchants. Burr won the first two cases. One can easily imagine Burr sitting in the courtroom on June 29, listening with great attention to the oral arguments in *Rutgers*, for he would have to counter them when he represented plaintiffs in his own cases.

Unlike Hamilton, whose orations in court sometimes carried him away, Burr was a careful and clever pleader, not an orator at all. In the courtroom, the impression he left was a striking one, of a man "of meagre form, but of an elegant symmetry . . . fair and transparent" with an "erect and dignified deportment . . . his presence is commanding . . . mild, firm, luminous and impressive." His eyes were hypnotic, deep-set, and "glow with all the ardor of venal fire, and scintillate with the most tremulous and tearful sensibility." Taciturn in company, when he spoke "his voice was clear, manly, and mellifluous." In court he proved a master of the quick riposte, the unexpected ambush, the relentless pursuit of an adversary on the run. He was elegant but not condescending to juries, not an orator but in person-to-person conversation highly persuasive. As Burr's biographer and younger friend Matthew Davis wrote of Burr's courtroom skills: "As a speaker, Colonel Burr was calm and persuasive. He was most remarkable for the power which he possessed of condensation. His appeals, whether to a court or a jury, were sententious and lucid. His speeches, generally, were argumentative, short, and pithy. No flights of fancy, no metaphors, no parade of impassioned sentences, are to be found in them."

So the bar class of 1782–1783 joined in the fray, young men sometimes working together on one side of the courtroom aisle, sometimes facing one another across the room. Hamilton and Burr would
be allies and opponents in the years to come, as would all of these
counselors. In some sense, this was to be the American way of law-
yering: a professional association of civility and study, fierce advocacy
and social intimacy. And so long as the parties to litigation accepted
the results of the litigation, there would not be another civil war.
When the two sides refused to accept legal settlements of their difference, another civil war came.

CHAPTER THREE

Rutgers v. Waddington in the Mayor's Court

If any legal institution could claim to represent the many strands of people and events in New York City's history from the founding of the city to 1784, it was the Mayor's Court. Created first by the Dutch in New Amsterdam as the court of schout, burgomeister, and schepens (essentially sheriff, mayor, and aldermen or council) for the city in 1665, it was refashioned by Lieutenant Governor General William Nicolls as the Mayor's Court. The transfer of title and jurisdiction went smoothly, especially given the fact that it came in wartime and was imposed by an invader. The second Anglo-Dutch War of 1664–1667 had brought Nicolls and a small fleet to the city, the center of the sprawling Dutch colony of New Netherlands. Nicolls spoke for the Duke of York, James Stuart, younger brother of King Charles II, whose province the Dutch lands became if his forces could occupy the land.

The Duke's Laws were not onerous, however, and the Mayor's Court transition was an example. Under English rule, its bench included four of the previous minders of the Dutch court, a policy of continuity and concession intended to attach the allegiance of the Dutch inhabitants to their new English rulers. The Dutch briefly reoccupied the city in 1673, during the last of the Anglo-Dutch wars, and the Mayor's Court reverted to its Dutch form. In 1674 the city and the court were once more English. Under the charter that Lieutenant Governor Thomas Dongan issued the City in 1686, the court lost its all-encompassing jurisdiction. The "recorder" of the city (its legal counsel) was added to the bench. In 1691 the Mayor's Court became a court of common pleas with one major difference from those in other colonies. Because the recorder sat on the bench with the mayor, the sheriff, and the aldermen, the court was always assured of having trained legal counsel at hand.

43

The history of the court in the eighteenth century paralleled that of the City. New York City had become a place of commerce where many peoples mingled. It was an entrepôt for English imports and the export of staples to England and foodstuffs to the West Indies. The people of the city practiced a variety of religions in a relatively tolerant cosmopolitanism even though the laws of the colony established the Church of England. Merchants dominated city governance. The Mayor's Court saw the underside of this activity, including disputes over bills of exchange, goods delivered but not paid for, payment for goods not delivered, and disputes over rent and lease terms. It was a busy court for the business of a busy city.

The court met in the City Hall at 28 Wall Street, a brick multi-story building that also housed the council chamber, the offices of the city officials, and a jail. The hall was the scene of the landmark 1735 trial of John Peter Zenger for a seditious libel of notorious royal governor William Cosby. Despite instructions to the contrary from Cosby's handpicked judge, the jury acquitted Zenger. Six years later, hundreds of slaves were tried there for conspiracy, petty treason, and arson. Though only a few were guilty, almost all confessed or were convicted. In 1765, a congress met there and framed colonial protests against the Stamp Act. The Stamp Act Congress was the precedent for the Continental Congress. The Declaration of Independence was read to a crowd from the City Hall balcony. The crowd then toppled the statue of King George III nearby. Three months later, City Hall became the nerve center of British occupying forces in the Revolutionary War. The Continental Congress moved to the City Hall in 1785, leaving behind the State House in Philadelphia. In 1788, after extensive repairs and expansion, the City Hall became Federal Hall, the first seat of the U.S. federal government. City Hall thus made and reflected the transition from local colonial to federal national governance in the space of a century.

To the Mayor's Court chamber on February 10, 1784, came *Rutgers*. Most business litigation is a tale of failing faith—a rupture in the normal course of commerce when one party decides that the other betrayed an agreement or acted badly. Common law pleading stuffed these tales of broken faith into formalistic straitjackets, narrowing issues so that they could be determined by a jury. But both parties in

{ *Chapter Three* }

the case agreed to proceed without a jury, and the depositions (written versions of oral accounts) that accompanied the case showed that the decision to sue by plaintiff and the disinclination to settle by defendant were not formalities. In particular, this case was riven with the animosities and mistrust that the war had spawned.

One side of this story comes to us from Waddington's affidavit. Following orders from the British authorities, from 1780 to 1783 all Loyalists and British occupiers of Patriot property paid rent on it for use by the city poorhouse and other charities. Benjamin Waddington and Evelyn Pierrepont had paid rent of £150 a year during this period. With word of the peace and the beginning of British forces' departure from the city, the British authorities had pressed Waddington, along with all the remaining British occupiers, to pay rent to returning Patriots who could show legal title to occupied properties. Anthony Rutgers, the widow Rutgers's son, then entered into conversation with Joshua Waddington for rent. The Trespass Act had not yet been passed. When it was passed, the tenor of the conversation between the two men over back rent changed. The act did not specify whether it was limited to, much less aimed at, the Loyalists who intended to remain in the state. Clearly it also applied to British subjects who wished to remain in the state. The political animus of the act is clear. Its impact on the two distinct communities of potential defendants was not.

Rutgers now demanded back rent and plainly was prepared to bring suit under the act to force Waddington to pay it. But Rutgers would not name a figure, perhaps waiting to see how other suits under the act would play out. Waddington then offered to turn over the property to the Rutgers family, the cost of the improvements made to the brewhouse acting as a substitute for back rent. Anthony Rutgers countered that the merchants should be dispossessed, get no recompense for the improvements, and pay a back rent of £1,200. This was not excessive if the basis was calculated on the seven years that the Rutgers family was unable to enter their property. On November 23, with the British now all but departed, a fire reduced the brewery to ashes. While the fire might have had a suspicious origin, brewhouses were very susceptible to fires and the slightest inattention to burning and boiling could result in a catastrophe. In any case, with the brewery's value now considerably reduced, Waddington returned the keys to what was left of the building to Rutgers. This settled the question of current rent. It did not settle the question of back rent.

In the eighteenth century, much civil litigation, particularly when the parties had not engaged in face-to-face negotiations and had no prior financial relationship, displayed a sense of wounded honor. The plaintiff concluded that the defendant had acted ignobly and could not be trusted to do the right thing. The defendant, contrariwise, concluded that the plaintiff was pulling a fast one, and must not be permitted to prevail. Litigation then ensued in both parties' attempt to restore a moral order as well as to force the other party to admit to misconduct. No doubt infuriated by the fire and suspecting it had a malicious origin, in February 1784 Anthony Rutgers filed an action in the Mayor's Court for £8000 back rent, over $1 million in modern exchange rates.

The exact date that papers beginning the suit were filed with the clerk is not clear, although it would probably have been February 10, when the clerk of the court and the sheriff attended and defendants were summoned. The £8000 was considerably more than the structure's worth, was over six times what Rutgers had originally asked, and did not correspond to past rent amounts. It was clearly a punitive rather than restorative figure, meant to crush the defendants for their wrongdoing and shift to them the costs of restoring the ruined structure rather than simply gaining reasonable back rent.

If the damages Rutgers sought exceeded by a good deal the amount at stake in most of the Trespass Act cases, the act provided that if the suit was initially brought in the Mayor's Court, it could be finally determined there. One could always appeal an adverse decision, of course, filing a writ of error with the clerk of the supreme court and putting up a bond to appear at its session in Albany. Such writs, bringing suits to a higher or appeals court, were commonly used. Certainly Hamilton was familiar with them from his part in the Hoffman case.

On the bench of the Mayor's court sat James Duane, the mayor and senior member, Richard Varick, the recorder (newly named) of the city, and the aldermen of the City's Common Council. Duane was a confident and experienced lawyer. Not every colonial or revolutionary judge was a lawyer, much less one with Duane's experience. Duane was born in New York, the son of an Anglo-Irish merchant, studied law with James Alexander, perhaps the foremost colonial New York attorney, and fit nicely within the circle around Robert R. Livingston, lord of the Livingston manor. Others in the circle were William Smith Jr., who would become a reluctant Loyalist and end his days as attorney general of Canada, and John Morin Scott. Duane married a daughter of Robert Livingston and served on the Committee of Sixty. The committee sent him to the Continental Congress, where, like William Livingston, Robert's younger brother, Duane was the most reluctant of rebels. Returned to New York, his allegiance to the Livingstons cemented his revolutionary credentials and provided a refuge for him and his wife when the British overran his home in the city. He was one of the authors of the new state constitution—perhaps the originator of its property holding requirements for voting. Clinton appointed him mayor of New York City in the winter of 1784, and on February 5, 1784, he accepted the post. In that capacity he presided over the Mayor's Court.

At Duane's side sat Varick. The recorder was another Kings College graduate, a lawyer, and former secretary to Washington. In 1788 Varick would become attorney general of the state. In the 1790s, he presided over the Mayor's Court. On February 21, 1784, Duane wrote to Varick congratulating him on being named recorder. The aldermen present, according to the Minutes of the Common Council for February 10, 1784, were Benjamin Blagge, Thomas Randall, John Broome, William W. Gilbert, William Nielson, Thomas Ivers, and Abraham P. Lott. Blagge was a former justice of the peace, the scion of a family going back generations in New York. Randall was early a colleague of Alexander McDougall and a successful merchant and privateer captain until the British occupation dislodged him. He returned from his New Jersey exile to the City with the coming of peace. Broome trained as a lawyer with William Livingston before the war but made his living as a merchant. He was a delegate to the convention that wrote the state constitution and served as president of the city's chamber of commerce and its treasurer in the 1780s. He would later serve as lieutenant governor under Morgan Lewis. Gilbert was a former cavalry officer during the war and one of the

City's leading silversmiths after it. His mansion in Greenwich Village was one of the finest on the island of Manhattan. After service on the Common Council he represented the city in the state assembly throughout the 1790s. Nielson was an overseas trader before the Revolution, owning a number of ships in the Irish trade in servants, seed, and pig iron. Ivers owned and operated a ropes works in the city, in part on lands formerly in possession of Loyalists. Lott served on the Committee of Sixty, represented the City in the State Assembly in 1781, when he was not leading a regiment of the militia as its colonel. These were not experienced lawyers, but they were men of parts and reputation.

The array of legal talent at the bar on both sides of the case was as formidable as the Mayor's Court bench. Plaintiff was represented by State Attorney General Egbert Benson. Benson, like other legal officials, also had a private practice. Benson was Elizabeth Rutgers's nephew. He was of Dutch New York ancestry and had had as distinguished a career thus far as any New York Patriot. He was also a resident of New York City, a lifelong bachelor, and in society a much esteemed invitee. Indeed, he was well known for his fondness for the delights of table, at which he joined in liveliness and gayety, according to James Kent, who served at the time as Benson's law clerk. Benson practiced law in the City for ten years before the breach with Great Britain, as well as in Duchess County on the Hudson. He served in the convention that wrote the state constitution, and from his seat in the assembly had a hand in writing the Loyalist Code provisions. He stepped down from the assembly in 1781 to serve as the attorney general of the state (multiple office holding, allowed under the colonial charters and in the English government, was forbidden by the state constitution), but he remained a resource for the lower house. Thus as counsel for Rutgers, he was in a uniquely privileged position to interpret legislative intent and textual meaning of the Trespass Act. He would later represent the state in the U.S. House of Representative and, briefly, serve on the Second Circuit federal court bench.

Joining him on the plaintiff's team were John Lawrence, William Wilcox, and Robert Troup. John Lawrence (the name is sometimes spelled Laurence) was an English immigrant who gained admission to the bar in 1775 after clerking in the city. There he met and married the daughter of Alexander McDougall and naturally cast his lot with the Patriot faction. With Hamilton, he served on the staff of General Washington as judge advocate general. It was not a pleasant post, for to him fell cases of desertion and misconduct in the ranks. He went to Congress in 1785 and was reelected to the new federal Congress in 1789. He joined the federal judiciary in 1794, replacing James Duane in the District of New York district court, resigned that position to serve in the U.S. Senate from 1796 to 1800, and thereafter resumed his private practice. His career in public office was scarcely inferior to Hamilton's, although nowhere did he demonstrate Hamilton's intellectual creativity.

William Wilcox was a City lawyer with a house on Nassau Street and a practice in the City. He graduated from the College of New Jersey in 1769, was admitted to the bar in the colony in 1774, and served on the staff of Revolutionary War general William Alexander, Lord Stirling. Wilcox died in 1816, never having held major public office. Robert Troup was ahead of Hamilton's class at Kings College and read law under John Jay. He served in the Battle of Long Island, where he was captured, then exchanged, and was present at the Saratoga surrender of General Burgoyne. Troup sat on various committees of Congress while continuing to practice law in Albany. Troup would serve on the ill-fated and short-lived circuit courts that the Judiciary Act of 1801 created and the Judiciary Act of 1802 abolished. He would become a sincere and trusted friend of Hamilton— for Hamilton's friendship was greatly prized and always reciprocated.

Burr's absence from Rutgers's team was noteworthy. He was in the city the entire time, often representing clients at the Mayor's Court, in fact at the very same sessions at which Lawrence filed the papers for *Rutgers*, on February 10 and his pleading on February 24. Burr's absence deserves attention because it suggests that the case had already become something of a political hot potato. He may have thought that the Trespass Act was a mistake, although, unlike Hamilton, Burr did not argue for its repeal when both men served in the assembly. It may be that the case had become so politically fraught that Burr thought it best to keep clear, as he was wont to avoid public displays of partisanship. In any case, his absence from the case did not harm his political fortunes. Burr was elected to the next session of the state assembly.

Sometime between February 10 and February 24, Hamilton agreed to defend Joshua Waddington. Hamilton certainly did not expect to face Benson. As late as February 18, he was seeking advice from Benson for the defense. Before he knew that Benson would be the opposing counsel, he wrote asking the attorney general's assistance. Waddington and his fellow British merchants wanted to remain in the colony. Hamilton added that this was the "general ground of our defense" and hoped that it would be "convenient" for Benson to be in court when the case came on. But Benson, like Hamilton, was a politician in a lawyer's skin, and he too had a larger purpose in taking the case. Like Hamilton, Benson wanted a public rather than just a private result—the defense of the legislature and its foremost position in the new republic. Burr, by contrast, kept his political cards closer to his chest. Were he chosen to represent Rutgers, the case, and its consequences, might have been entirely altered.

On February 24, Hamilton formally told the court that he had been retained by Joshua Waddington. The two-week period between the filing of the case and the notice of attorney participation was set out in the court's rules of procedure. Hamilton was not coming in late. In fact, Hamilton was counsel of record for the defense in two other suits Rutgers brought against British merchants, so he had more than a little at stake in these proceedings. Hamilton would later represent Loyalists in seven other Trespass Act cases in 1784 and 1785.

Already representing Waddington were Henry Brockholst Livingston and Morgan Lewis. Lewis, like Livingston and Burr, was a graduate of the College of New Jersey, and the "social capital" of such connections carried into domestic and professional spheres. Trained by John Jay, Lewis passed the bar in 1782. He married into the Livingston family, wedding the sister of Robert R. Livingston. Lewis would serve in the state assembly, as attorney general of the state in 1791–1792, and rise from associate to chief justice of the New York Supreme Court. From 1804 to 1807 Lewis was governor of the state, defeating his old colleague Burr and perhaps precipitating the Hamilton-Burr duel (after Hamilton played a decisive role in denying the office to Burr). The Waddington team entered the profession at the same time, were all part of the Livingston circle, and were all destined for higher posts. In years to come, this small and able coterie of lawyers passed public office around like the dishes at a family style dinner. Allies at times, opponents at other times, the reputation of the judges and counsel in *Rutgers* gave the case even more importance than the issues at stake.

———

Hamilton, no stranger to controversy and never one to avoid it, had already ramped up the stakes of *Rutgers* with an open letter, really a mini-pamphlet, on the state's proposed Alien Act and the treatment of the Loyalists in general. He signed it Phocion, the name of an ancient Athenian statesman nicknamed "the good." The letter appeared early in January (the exact date is uncertain), while the debate over the alien bill raged—the legislature passed it but the Council of Revision blocked it. In the meantime, important Loyalist figures were either leaving the city or had left, a prospect that Hamilton feared. *Phocion* was thus a preview of arguments that Hamilton planned to use to defend British (alien) occupiers and former Loyalist occupiers of Patriot property, and in a way an advertisement for his services in defending such suits. It appeared before Lawrence filed the papers in *Rutgers* on February 10, but Hamilton undoubtedly knew about the quarrel and the impending suit. He may have been approached about defending Pierrepont and the Waddingtons already, or he may have been angling for the job.

The departure of British merchants and Loyalists, along with the elections in New York City over the course of the winter, spurred Hamilton's temper, as the opening passages of the letter demonstrated. (When pushed to the limit of his very limited patience by insult or dispute, Hamilton was wont to offer to take on the lot of his opponents, one by one.) Hamilton warned that "a few heated and inconsiderate spirits" were playing on the "passions" of the people, offering "the most inflammatory and pernicious doctrines" to "trample on the rights of the subject." "The subject" was an old term—Hamilton should have said the citizen, but the rights in question were also old: the right to own, use, acquire, and transfer one's property. The advocates of the alien bill claimed that they acted in the Whig spirit, the spirit of the Revolution (though Hamilton did not use that term). Instead, they were agents of "revenge, cruelty, persecution, and perfidy." This was the very language, in the same tone of offended decency, that the Loyalists had used when they were driven from their property outside of the City. Hamilton did not quote it, for obvious reasons, but he leaned on it for support. The Alien Act would have disenfranchised the Loyalists, to Hamilton's mind a violation of the state constitution, barring such disenfranchisement except "by the law of the land." This did not amount to a temporary majority in a popular legislative body passing a law, but by due process of law—trial in a court and conviction for a crime. The legislature had, during the war, attainted by name and so disenfranchised leading Loyalists, but even those enactments provided for regular legal process for those not named. Now there was a treaty, and that treaty, aided and abetted by "natural justice, and fundamental principle of law and liberty" barred such legislative license.

The rest of the letter read as a brief might read in defense of an individual affected by the Alien Act. That act did not yet exist, but Hamilton was ready for it with a three-pronged attack. The first lay in the treaty; the second lay in natural law; the third lay in a novel legal argument—what amounted to a "best use" of property doctrine. Hamilton rejected a form of legislative intent analysis, where the text of a law (here the treaty) is read in light of the debates on its ratification. Instead, he relied on what today would be a kind of plain text parsing, laying the various clauses of the treaty against one another, "the sound and ingenious construction of the two articles" concerning Loyalist treatment, to conclude that the British did not abandon the rights of their former allies in America. The treaty's terms would be defeated if it allowed the states to deny to the former Loyalists the protections of government and the rights of citizens.

Hamilton's facts were not entirely accurate, for some Loyalists occupied and enjoyed the profitable use of property that did not belong to them before the British occupied the city. He swept this fact away by arguing the general principle, his second prong, that no citizen could be deprived of the rights that other citizens possessed unless they were guilty of a crime. Adherence to the crown during the war was a crime according to the Alien Act, but no Loyalist had yet been convicted in a court of law under the Alien Act because it was not yet passed. Thus the beauty of Hamilton's argument, a kind of bold circularity: you cannot lose your rights unless you are convicted of a crime under the laws of the state, but you cannot be tried until those laws are in force. To top it off (and close the circle): the treaty forbade such laws criminalizing anything done "on account of the war." Some remarks in passing on how much Britain had surrendered in the treaty, in particular the western lands gained from France in the Treaty of 1763, the Great Lakes ports, and the fisheries on the Grand Banks of Newfoundland, demonstrated how generous the former imperial rulers had been. "A man of honesty, not intoxicated with passion" would "blush" at the suggestion that a generous interpretation of the treaty terms regarding the Loyalists was hardly a great concession.

Hamilton's next subject concerned the treaty-making powers of Congress and how these limited the sovereignty of the state of New York. While the legislature had the power to make laws for the state's inhabitants and their property, only "political jugglers" would deny that the treaty-making power lay in Congress. That power outweighed the internal police powers of the state. Here Hamilton opened an argument that would appear over and over in American constitutional jurisprudence. It ran through the federalism compromise at the Constitutional Convention, reared its head in the debates over slavery and secession, took on new forms in the Gilded Age battles over state regulation of labor conditions, ran all through the Jim Crow and desegregation cases, and has emerged once more in gun control. Hamilton was there at the creation, but as there was no federal Constitution, he could not base the argument on its Supremacy Clause. Instead, he looked to history. History offered many cases of mutual indemnity of agents of former warring powers. But did indemnity from prosecution also restore adherents to the other side their privileges as citizens of their own nation? Hamilton did not say.

Did Congress have the authority to bind the states to the terms of the treaty? "Equity and prudence" dictated yes, but that was conditional on the state governments recognizing that resistance would cost the new nation all its diplomats had won. The British would not leave their frontier posts until the terms of the treaty were fully satisfied. Some of these terms, including the payment of prewar debts owed British merchants, were not in the hands of the state governments, though in 1790 Secretary of the Treasury Hamilton would press for assumption of the state debts by the federal government and federal government's payment of its own debts. It would be years before Congress agreed to a watered-down version of payment of private debts owed to British merchants. Worse still, delay in compliance with the treaty would cost the new nation esteem and trust among the other nations of Europe. Hamilton was not a diplomat, but his friend and patron John Jay was, and anyone reading John Jay's reports to Congress as the secretary of foreign affairs would see where Hamilton got the idea.

The natural law portion of the letter was an attempt to find in the evolving contemporary idea of the law of nations, a subject of growing interest among Enlightenment intellectuals, a basis for the equitable treatment of aliens. According to "natural justice, and a fundamental principle of law and liberty," no class of persons should be disfavored by the law, Hamilton argued. Individuals in the class might suffer for their actions, but the entire category should not be subject to unfair treatment.

> If the legislature can disfranchise any number of citizens at pleasure by general descriptions, it may soon confide all the votes to a small number of partizens, and establish an aristocracy or an oligarchy; if it may banish at discretion all those whom particular circumstances render obnoxious, without hearing or trial, no man can be safe, nor know when he may be the innocent victim of a prevailing faction. The name of liberty applied to such a government would be a mockery of common sense.

The third prong of the argument hinted that the best policy to insure the nation's prosperity was to allow property to find its best use. This is a doctrine that most scholars attribute to the early portion of the next century, but here, as in so much of his thinking, Hamilton was ahead of the pack. Best use meant that the British merchants were adding to the sum of utility by putting the brewhouse back into operation. An abandoned structure or even a temporary barracks for the British forces did not promote commerce, add to the job pool, or produce goods for public consumption nearly as well as a working brewhouse. "Every merchant or trader has an interest in the aggregate mass of capital or stock in trade; that what he himself wants in capital, he must make up in credit; that unless there are others who possess large capital, this credit cannot be had, and that in the diminution of the general capital of the state, commerce will decline, and his own prospects of profit will diminish."

In closing, Hamilton played the class war card. He recognized that some of the appeal of the statute lay not in the war years, but in a deeper animosity against the wealthy. By portraying the Loyalists as a small body of rich men, their opponents sought to rally the small merchant, the mechanic (laborer), and the craftsman. Hamilton had an easy reply: a rising tide raised all boats. The wealthy would provide jobs, infuse the economy with capital, and establish commerce on a sound foundation. It was the same argument he would make for a national bank when he was secretary of the treasury in 1791.

The form of the letter combined the rhetorical excess of Patriot pamphlet literature of the crisis period with the precise reasoning of the legal brief. This was a natural combination for Hamilton, as he had contributed to both genres already. Many of the leading revolutionary pamphleteers, for example John Adams, John Dickinson, Daniel Dulany, James Otis Jr., and Thomas Jefferson, were practicing lawyers. To the combination of the genres Hamilton added his own personal touch—an impatient and sharp-tongued refusal to conciliate his opponent or mollycoddle his readers. To some extent, Hamilton's immoderation was excusable, for he labeled the Alien Act the work of a partisan faction and the language of political partisanship in that day bordered on the defamatory. At the same time, one should not forget that Hamilton was swinging away at the majority of the state legislature, a big target but a dangerous one for a man with political ambitions. Signing the letter with a pseudonym might protect against the enmity of some of the bill's advocates, but the pseudonym offered little more concealment of his identity than Adam's fig leaf.

Why then the intemperate tone? Election of the City government was concluded by the time that *Phocion* was published. Hamilton's review of the arguments on both sides could not influence that election. Election of the legislators was already past. But as the Alien Act was still not law, and the City government would play a major part in it would it become law, one may surmise that the audience for Hamilton's remarks was not the electorate, but the mayor and aldermen—the very same group before which he would soon plead Waddington's cause. One can then read *Phocion* as an anticipatory quasi-legal brief in *Rutgers*—anticipatory because the pleading in the case had not begun and quasi because the Alien Act was not the subject of the on-coming litigation.

———

Pleading in the Mayor's Court by this time followed the rules of common law "writ pleading." In writ pleading, one fit one's claim to one of the available formats, the number and language of writs having been fixed in the common law. One simply paid one's attorney to fill in the blank spaces in the writ and present it to the clerk of the court along with the fee for filing. Your opponent was notified by another kind of writ, and responded. Thus the legal contest was joined. Brought to court by the original writ and the writ ordering the defendant to appear, trial allowed both sides to present their case, and the judge or the jury determined which set of facts seemed most plausible. Sue under the wrong writ, and one faced dismissal of the case.

"Trespass" was one of these writs, but it was used to begin a suit for negligent harms ("trespass on the case," today a tort); for carrying off goods not belonging to one ("trespass de bonis asportatis"); entering onto another's land to contest title to the land ("trespass de quare clausum fregit"); and assault on one's person or destruction of one's property ("trespass vi et armis"), rather than seek back rent directly. Were one suing under the common law in a common law court, one would have to bring *Rutgers* under the trespass quare clausum fregit, alleging that the occupiers had used force to deny Elizabeth Rutgers the benefits of her property, to which Waddington could reply that he had acted under the authority and indeed the command of the law (that is, the lawful British authorities). Recall that the state constitution had left common law pleading intact in the state courts.

Hamilton told Benson that he thought the case would come up

in four or five weeks. By that time, both sides would have filed briefs and had the chance to reply to one another. Lawrence would have time to amend his brief to include the vital clause in the Trespass Act barring the defense of military command, a course that Hamilton's letter to Benson might have prompted. The exchange in court came sooner than Hamilton expected, however, a mere two weeks after he had written to Benson.

Lawrence filed for the widow Rutgers and her son on February 10, 1784, the first time the Mayor's Court's clerk would docket cases for the new session. The court had proposed new rules for pleading, though Lawrence's "narrative" does not seem to have fit any of the categories. The old Mayor's Court was constantly altering its rules of process, admitting that each former set of rules had proved ineffective. The old rules were less formal. Now the court adopted rules much like any common law court for summoning witnesses. If a party failed to appear, the sheriff was authorized to compel performance, taking bail to insure appearance, and failing that, taking possession of property for failing to plead. Even the small claims courts in the colonies had become more English in the years before the war, as English rule books and English-trained lawyers appeared in the courtroom.

Hamilton thought about removing the case to the chancellor's court. That colonial court of equity survived in the new constitution. Its presiding officer was the chancellor and he was none other than Robert R. Livingston. As a member of the Council of Revision, he had blocked passage of the Alien Act, and he was in sympathy with Hamilton's general position. One leading scholar of the affair has suggested that removal to the court of equity would have given the defense a better chance to win the case. There pleading was far simpler. Following English rules of equity, a simple claim was made stating the reasons for the claim and the relief desired. The court ordered depositions taken and evidence produced and then rendered a decision. There were grounds for a defense of his clients in the equitable concept of clean hands. Waddington had paid rent to the British government in the city. He occupied the premises under that government's order and fulfilled his obligations to it. He thus could come into equity with clean hands. This answer to the Rutgers' claim circumvented the Trespass Act's provision denying the defense of military necessity. The case was not removed, however, as the amount Rutgers sought was far larger than Hamilton had anticipated, and there would have been a question of jurisdiction, as the Trespass Act provided that a case brought in a local court was to stay in that court until it was concluded. (One might even think that one reason for the extravagance of the Rutgers' claim was to keep the case out of the chancellor's court.)

In any case, Hamilton decided to use the suit to make a larger point about the confederation and the union. It was a project he had in mind before he agreed to represent Waddington. The previous December, Hamilton had joined Lewis, Duane, and Varick in writing to Thomas Mifflin, the president of the Congress. In the letter, the New York lawyers, "Being concerned as Council for a number of persons, who, since the annunciation of the provisional treaty have been indicted under the confiscation laws of this state for the part they are supposed to have taken in the late war, we are induced at the desire of our clients and in their behalf, to apply to Congress through your Excellency for an exemplification of the definitive treaty."

With Duane and Varick on the bench, Hamilton could no longer formally seek their support for the former Loyalists' cause. Setting aside the irony of Hamilton revealing to Benson how he intended to plead, one notes that Hamilton was using the case to build a network of allies for his campaign to rehabilitate the Loyalists. One can infer from the brief he wrote for the Mayor's Court that winning in the chancellor's court might aid his client, but winning by showing that the Trespass Act violated the treaty, hence the supremacy of the confederation government over the state government in matters of foreign affairs, was the bigger fish that Hamilton wanted to land. He almost certainly knew that Duane had a similar preference, or at least similar goals.

We do not know the precise authorship of the various briefs for the plaintiff, but since Lawrence filed the case, it may not be unreasonable to assume he was the first to argue for the widow Rutgers. It may be that Hamilton's *Phocion*, a preview of his line of defense, constrained Lawrence's options. If that were so, then Hamilton had set the terms of the legal contest even before Lawrence submitted his initial pleading—or not, as the issues seemed pretty straightforward from the outset. Notes for Hamilton's brief were found in his papers, suggesting that they were his own. Missing is the brief that Duane wanted submitted to the court after oral argument on June 29. While Hamilton might have had a copy of this, the final version should also have been in the records of the court or in Duane's papers, but it did not appear in either. It did, however, appear in substance in Duane's opinion, delivered on August 27.

———

Hamilton by now had even more on his plate than preparation of his oral argument and written brief in *Rutgers*. An anonymous critic of the *Phocion* letter had published a pamphlet, and Hamilton rushed to reply in print. *Mentor's Reply to Phocion's Letter* was a burr beneath Hamilton's saddle. *Mentor's Reply* must have appeared no later than March 1784 because Hamilton's second *Phocion* letter, a rejoinder to Mentor, was published in April. Mentor had to be an able polemicist himself, for he composed and published his essay within a few months of Hamilton's first letter. Hamilton too was a fast and furious scribbler, but had to have some time to pen and arrange for publication of his reply. Hamilton's reply referred to a bill nearing passage in the state legislature at the end of March. This also puts Mentor's appearance no later than the middle of March.

Mentor belongs in the same line of works as the *Phocion* letters. It is a mixture of revolutionary pamphleteering and legal brief, although its literary quality bespeaks a pen not used to such writings. The essay itself is a kind of amicus (friend of the court) brief in *Rutgers*. Like the closing portion of Hamilton's letter, *Mentor's Reply* introduced policy arguments, then a novel feature of legal briefs.

Mentor decried Phocion as too pompous, vain, and warm of temper to be taken seriously. By contrast, Mentor promised not to clutter his pages with "learned form, or to plague [the reader]" with "frequent quotations from the works of the dead, to show his own great reading" as, supposedly, had Hamilton. Plainly, Mentor knew the identity of Phocion, "an eminent servant of the republic in establishing her independency, but one as having been flattered by success in the early stage of life, has acquired too much respect for its own capacity and too much contempt for that of others"—a somewhat uncharitable but not entirely inaccurate portrait of Hamilton.

Although Phocion relied on citation and authority, Mentor offered to simply state his case. Mentor's refutation of Hamilton's arguments was simple—first, there was no basis for them in the text of the treaty. Nothing in it proposed any provision for giving the Loyalists back what they had voluntarily abjured. Second, the Loyalists were not aliens to the country, newly come, and Congress could not by treaty make them aliens whose rights the laws of war protected. They were enemies who in time of civil war adhered to Britain. Any truly sovereign state must have within its powers the prevention of future mischief from such men. "The treaty, which justice and honor forbid us to violate, does not, even upon so liberal a construction . . . as Phocion would give it, debar the states from making laws that may be salutary to the government, and advantageous to the people, though in their consequences they may operate against the interest of the subjects of England." Only justice and honor, not law, prevented New York from violating the letter of the treaty. The state was a sovereignty, resting on the sovereignty of the people. The Confederation Congress was not a sovereignty and rested on the consent of the states. If New York had agreed not to take vengeance upon their persons, it need not agree to restore them to the very privileges which they had cast away. Reason, prudence, and experience had taught states to quarantine or exile those who had plotted against the lawful government.

To this Mentor added that "the opinion of the people" in a republic must prevail over its former enemies' claims. He warned that some among the former enemies to the state were again intriguing to positions of power within it. They were "mal-contents" who would pervert the Revolution and undermine republicanism. For, "in a republic, the people are their own governors. A republican government must take its shape from the opinion of the people." This was precisely the argument that defenders of the Trespass Act had made a year earlier, and prior to that, the argument that the county committees had offered in defense of their harassment of the Loyalists.

Mentor closed with a paean to the husbandman and the manufacturer and a warning against the overseas trader and their friends abroad. From such men could only come corruption of republican virtue. It was "a plain and simple truth . . . that the riches of a nation are derived from the cultivation of its land and its manufactures" and "I would encourage husbandmen and manufacturers to come to the country, and discourage traders." Merchants were but middlemen between the producer and the consumer, and to be closely watched. Surely, Mentor implied, no one needed to be told that the Waddingtons fit the latter description.

Nineteenth-century historians credited revolutionary surgeon Isaac Ledyard with authorship of *Mentor's Reply*, but the attribution is uncertain. The editors of the *Hamilton Papers*, in a note to Hamilton's second *Phocion* letter, explained, "Given Ledyard's obscurity and the fact that he and Hamilton were political allies in 1792 and presumably earlier, there is little reason to assume that he wrote *Mentor's Reply*." By his own admission in a short treatise he wrote the same year on the handling of matter in Pope's essays, *An Essay on Matter*, Ledyard was hardly likely to challenge Hamilton so swiftly or surely. For "The author finds his indisposition so obstinate, as to make him despair, at least for a long time, of recovering that health of body and vigor of mind, required" for writing *Mentor*. In later life, Ledyard would seek the assistance of poet and journalist Philip Freneau in composing an edition of the life and letters of his explorer cousin John Ledyard, a task that a man of literary inclination and ability might not have needed assistance to accomplish.

Might it then be that Mentor was not Ledyard at all, but a lawyer not employed in the cause but strongly attached to the interests of the plaintiff in *Rutgers*? All of Mentor's arguments—the absence of a command to respect Loyalist property in the treaty, the sovereignty of the state, and the authority of the people to do what was in their best interest—were those that Burr must have made to represent plaintiffs in Trespass Act cases. The style of argument was also Burr's—plain, to the point, and persuasive. Burr represented former Loyalists and British citizens in court. He was never an ideologue. But in his politics he leaned a little to the interests of his adopted state and against those of the confederation. Unfortunately, the trunk with Burr's manuscripts and correspondence from his early days as a lawyer was in the possession of his daughter Theodosia when she disappeared at sea in 1813. Only a handful of letters survive, none from the period when Mentor was at work.

There is no internal evidence in Hamilton's reply to Mentor that he knew for certain the identity of its author. Instead, he scoffed that Mentor must be a mere partisan (knowing that partisan politics were never fully acceptable in the political thinking of the day). Such men wanted to acquire "power and profit" for themselves, to which end they would "overturn the foundations of public and private security." In short, Mentor and his crew were radicals whose ideas reflected "party intrigue" and "personal animosity" rather than the will of the people. This are-so, am-not, sort of refutation ran all through the second *Phocion* letter and did not introduce anything of particular worth.

Hamilton could have spared himself the effort, but it was not in his nature to let a challenge pass without an answer—not if, as he might have suspected, the author was not an obscure Long Island surgeon, but a prospective rival in New York and national politics. The fact that he replied along with the tenor of his reply hints that he regarded Mentor as someone who could not be ignored. Some historians have characterized this era as a political culture of honor, in which gentlemen (or those aspiring to be gentlemen) used words as dueling pistols. Little did Hamilton know that this attitude toward political calumny—slinging it and dodging it—would be the death of him.

In his reply to Mentor, Hamilton argued that citizenship was not a matter of voluntary allegiance, but of actual domicile. Everyone in the newly independent United States' borders when independence was declared was a citizen of the state where they lived. As a matter of fact, this was not true. Slaves did not become citizens because of their domicile. Residence in a state did not render Indians its citizens. But Hamilton immediately went from the general principle to the specific: "The inhabitants of the southern district [i.e., New York City and Long Island] before they fell under the power of the British army, were as much citizens of the state as the inhabitants of other parts of it." They remained citizens unless "divested of it." Such loss of citizenship could only be the result of conviction of a crime. To assume anything else would "convert misfortune [of remaining within British lines] into guilt." Now had come the time to "correct the exuberances of opinion" that automatically excluded from citizenship those who were simply residents of British-controlled territory. To accomplish this Hamilton launched into a complex parsing of the treaty provisions. In the end, he concluded that the treaty, rightly read, protected the latter sort of person. They were not turned into aliens by their allegiance to the old royal government, but remained what they had been, citizens of New York.

Hamilton did offer one telling argument to unpack the importance of the treaty. It had nothing to do with the logic chopping he employed elsewhere in the essay. Instead, he proposed to read the treaty in terms of its initial reception in the United States, in effect, in terms of the spirit of the treaty rather than its letter. "Every man, by appealing to his own bosom, would reflect" that the treaty as a whole entreated Americans to readmit the Loyalists who wanted to belong to the new nation. Actually, that was true of Hamilton and many others who had fought against the British. But it was not true of many other revolutionary politicians who carried a grudge. Hamilton cited the baby steps taken in this direction during the late election for the city government. Everyone willing to take the oath, whether or not they had resided within the occupied city, was allowed to vote. Surely Mentor could see that no evil had followed. The alternative, declaring everyone who adhered to the British to be guilty of treason, as hinted in *Mentor's Reply* as the alternative to the Trespass Act approach, was unthinkable even to the Trespass Act's defenders. "Making peace" in this way was neither sentimental nor partisan, it was Hamilton's way of saying it was time to move on from civil war to civil peace.

Hamilton had prepared his arsenal of arguments well, turning what had been a matter of private law into a subject of public policy. It was a pattern that he would adopt in later years—using his office or the printer's office to lay out plans for the government. The vision was already there—a strong national government behind which stood men of property; an orderly and sound world safe from the swirling risks that commerce in the new nation (and Hamilton himself) faced. And now he had to win *Rutgers v. Waddington*.

Hamilton answered Lawrence's pleading on April 21, in a somewhat abbreviated fashion. His central argument was that the British merchants were British subjects occupying a property in British territory under the orders of the British military officer, and those, in turn, according to the laws of war. "All political connection" between the states of the United States and the British government "was and ought to be totally dissolved." They were thus not subject to the Trespass Act because the laws of war provided those conditions as a defense against the Trespass Act, whatever the Trespass Act may have (and did) say to the contrary. The fact that they remained in the city after the British had decamped, that the British had told them to pay rent to Rutgers after the treaty was initialed, and that they offered to pay rent, did not diminish any of their defense to the claim of back rent. All this (at least Hamilton's reading of) the treaty confirmed. Lawrence demurred to (rejected) Hamilton's reply, and Hamilton repeated it, thus bringing the case to court.

Between April 21 and June 29, Hamilton prepared a series of documents. The first was a draft to remove the case to the chancellor's court that he did not file with its clerk. The second was the outline of a brief, which the third filled in with legal citations and the fourth tidied up; the fifth was a set of notes for oral response on the 29th taken while Benson made his oral argument (since lost) to the court. The last document was prepared for appeal of the suit to the state supreme court and must have been prepared after Lawrence either filed or made known his intention to file a writ of error to appeal the case. (Hamilton mentioned the writ in a letter to Thomas Jefferson in 1792, hinting that both sides actually did file the paperwork with the clerk of the supreme court. The context of that letter is discussed below.) Only the first of these documents was headed Rutgers and Waddington, but the content of the others leave little doubt that they were prepared in the course of the case. Because the briefs were not dated, there is no certain way to determine their order, but internal evidence suggests the above.

While the canons of scholarly editing may direct that each document be treated separately, and in the most detailed reproduction of the documents they are, here the account of Hamilton's middle three drafts are combined in what amounts to a concordance. There is great danger in doing this when the authenticity and the authorship of the documents are doubtful and their order may be important to understanding an event. In one notorious case a consonance of three quite disparate and questionable accounts of a slave revolt into a single document concealed and misconstrued the way in which testimony was taken. The resulting volume was so riddled with errors that its author and the press agreed to take the work out of print.

That is not the case here, however. There is no question that Hamilton was the author. All of the arguments that appear were already tested, albeit in more general form, in the *Phocion* letters. Hamilton himself would combine them in the written brief he submitted to the court on July 29 and which appears in Duane's opinion. (Although unusual, in this case Duane apparently asked counsel for both parties to submit written briefs after they had argued the case. He used these in the composition of his own opinion.)

The foremost interpreter of Hamilton's performance on this occasion, Julius Goebel, suggests that Hamilton's presentation took the form of a series of aphorisms, short bursts of argument and authority. Like a noteworthy analysis of the diacritical marks in the reading copy Thomas Jefferson prepared of the draft Declaration of Independence, one can find in the draft notes for Hamilton's oral argument certain indications of emphasis. Hamilton used the iconic symbol of a pointing finger to point to key passages, alphabetically arrayed large capital letters to show the sequence of argument, and briefly referenced authorities in the margins for purposes of citation.

The substance of Hamilton's briefs can be reconstructed from the documents in his papers. The first brief, an argument for removal to the chancellor's court, featured the following key argument: "A court of common law considers only whether the action be founded in law—a court of equity adds another consideration, whether it be just and fair in the plaintiff to insist on the action." What was Hamilton driving at? A party seeking equity must enter the court with clean hands. To get equity one must do equity. Waddington had asked Rutgers to name a rent. Rutgers refused to do so for nearly a year. Then Rutgers demanded possession of the property, including all the improvements and repairs that Waddington had made, and a lump sum payment of nearly £8000 for back rent. A court of equity might well see this as unfair—vituperative, inconsiderate, and harsh. It was a nice point, but the case stayed in the Mayor's Court.

The next three briefs were prepared for the Mayor's Court. Hamilton opened by noting that the importance of the case lay not only in its correct settlement, but "from the numbers [of law cases] depending on the same principle and from its influence on the national character." Whatever did Hamilton mean by "national character"? The matter was a state case, in a state court, under state law. One must remember that the notes we have are Hamilton's shorthand. A clue to his thinking lay not in the notes, but in a letter he wrote four years earlier to James Duane. At that time, Hamilton had become disenchanted with his role as aide-de-camp. He was getting ready to leave his military career behind and was turning his thoughts to politics. "Agreeably to your request and my promise I sit down to give you my ideas of the defects of our present system, and the changes necessary to save us from ruin. They may perhaps be the reveries of a projector rather than the sober views of a politician. You will judge of them, and make what use you please of them." There followed a mini-treatise of the sort that Hamilton would repeat throughout the 1780s, including his contributions to the Federalist Papers.

According to Hamilton, Congress had too little power and the states too much "liberty" to pursue their own ends to the detriment of the national interest. As Washington's aide-de-camp Hamilton had seen a nation at war. He recognized its potential and its limitations. The latter derived from states' short-sighted self-interest. At key moments, they had removed their militias from the Continental line; failed to provide their requisitions on time; and embraced disunion when unity was critical.

By contrast, Hamilton thought that the survival of the nation depended on a Congress with the inherent power to "preserve the republic from harm." Such a loose construction of the Articles of Confederation (to use a term that would become the watchword of Hamilton's tenure as secretary of the treasury) was essential to "complete sovereignty." For only with such "undefined powers" could the Congress cope with novel situations when necessity demanded.

Thus "the confederation itself is defective and requires to be altered." The states had too much power over the military and the purse. Hamilton did not argue for a singular centralized imperial authority. Such a government would endanger the liberties for which the Patriots fought. But Congress must have powers "competent" for public "exigencies"; it must have an energetic and efficient administration; and above all, it must have the power to raise a revenue. For the sinew of government was its power to tax. Only a Congress that had its own revenue could protect the property of individuals—or enforce the treaty provisions on a reluctant state.

In this closing passage, Hamilton intimated how the case for a robust reading of the treaty powers of Congress fit into an even more fundamental conception of a national political economy. The reintegration of the Loyalists into the political and economic life of the nation and a welcome to British merchants who wanted to do business in America under the treaty was wise policy for both New York and the United States. It would promote European investment in America.

These were the ideas that *Phocion* applied to the threat of an Alien Act and they were the ideas on which Hamilton planned to defend Waddington. The obstacle in 1784 was not quite the same as in 1780. In 1780, the Articles of Confederation had not yet been ratified, the war seemed endless, the debt was piling up, and Congress was staggering. By the opening of 1784, Congress had achieved a military victory and a very favorable peace settlement. New York sovereignty, which in 1780 was not yet assured, in 1784 was fully vindicated. Thus the relationship between the state and the confederation government had changed. Hamilton insisted that the new relationship must be based on mutual trust and the key to that trust was for New York to accede to the fullest deployment of the treaty within its borders. In other words, New York would have to interpret its own laws according to the precepts of the law of nations that undergirded the treaty. For Hamilton, if the question was one between "the subjects of two independent nations . . . the law to be applied was the law of nations." Hamilton knew that the state of New York had not adopted the law of nations whole (saving for itself such exceptions as it deemed necessary), but he opined that the law of nations was the law of nature adapted to the use of states, and the latter "is universally binding on the conscience" of those states' governing agencies.

So far, nothing in the brief touched the Trespass Act in general, much less the act's exclusion of the military necessity defense, but Hamilton was inching his way there. He argued that the obligations that the law of war imposed on nations were embodied in the positive law of each nation. Hamilton correctly continued that the constitution of the state of New York had adopted such of the common law as was practiced in 1775, and—here was his leap of faith—that the common law included the law of nations.

This assumption rested not on positive law, that is, a statute of Parliament or a decision of the English High courts, much less on the statutes of the state of New York. It rested on English jurisprudence, the theoretical analysis and scholarship of law, and in particular (since Hamilton was quoting from it), the foremost of these scholarly treatises, William Blackstone's *Commentaries on the Laws of England* (1765–1769). Blackstone was widely read and greatly respected among colonial and revolutionary lawyers. He spent a good deal of time in the first of his four volumes on the subject of natural law and he did assume that the common law rested upon natural law. Blackstone asserted that natural law came before all positive law; common law "derived its force" from natural law; natural law was binding all over the globe; positive law that contradicted natural law was invalid; and that the law of nations was derived from natural law.

But Blackstone rejected the idea that the right of property rested on natural law or its stepchild, the law of nations. Reason, practicality, and practice had created this right rather than a body of foreign precepts. Occupation of a piece of property conferred a temporary right. Mutual convenience extended this right. But only the intervention of the nation state made property use and ownership into a legal right that could be defended in a court of law. It was municipal law, the rule or civil principle laid down by the sovereign, that men must obey.

If one took Blackstone as one's authority, obedience to the commands of the state (for him, England, in *Rutgers* the state of New York) was the logical outcome of natural law, including the power of the state to set rules for ownership of property, payment of rents, and all other rules for property within its territory. Blackstone argued that only insofar as the English courts adopted precepts from natural law was it binding in England, or its colonies. In other words, civil conduct rested on municipal law and the municipal law in question in *Rutgers v. Waddington* was the Trespass Act. Hamilton was on shaky ground if he stood with Blackstone.

Blackstone went further. Although under the law of nations the person of an ambassador was safe from prosecution, if an ambassador of a foreign nation committed a heinous crime in England, his immunity stemmed not from natural law, but from an act of Parliament. Only when English positive law provided for diplomatic immunity would it be granted. Hamilton simply ignored this distinction; whether or not he understood it, he had to ignore it, as it undercut his argument. True, Blackstone thought that Parliament was supreme; but the members of the New York State legislature thought that their sovereignty was supreme, too.

Hamilton's attempt to find support in Blackstone rested on the English jurist's own argument in a 1764 lawsuit. In it, he averred that parliamentary statutes had merely reduced to formula what the common law already held: the law of nations was binding in English courts. But Blackstone continued that incorporation was selective on a case-by-case and issue-by-issue basis. Thus the immunity of ambassadors and other diplomatic personnel was ensured, as were rules for captures at sea, because Parliament incorporated these international law concepts. The English courts and Parliament were not subject to international law except as they bound themselves to be. Once again, just at the point where Blackstone might have been cited in support for Hamilton's position on the law of nations, the English jurisprudent stopped.

Hamilton's second strand of argument boldly asserted that the laws of war did apply to New York. Whether or not the laws of war applied in 1784, or affected persons and property after peace was concluded, they applied in the city from 1776 to 1783, he insisted, and Waddington was merely obeying the law of war in occupying property under military control. Hamilton cited the law of war dictum that "vacant and derelict property by the most civilized practice of nations is appropriated by the captor."

Hamilton did not stop there. He tried to convince the court that Congress's ratification of the treaty implied a general amnesty. This amnesty applied to all who supported the crown in the late conflict (i.e., voiding the acts of attainder and any prosecutions for treason) and their property (including that already confiscated and in the case of New York the parcels sold at auction). But the brewhouse was never the property of the Waddingtons—that is, occupancy did not confer legal title. Nor had the Waddingtons ever asserted that possession gave them such title. If the treaty voided the Trespass Act, it must be through a more complicated mechanism than the general amnesty provision.

Hamilton thus carried on to argue that courts were bound to void the Trespass Act if it violated either the law of nations or the treaty provisions. He cited Lord Chief Justice Edward Coke's dictum in *Dr. Bonham's Case* (1610; 77 Eng. Rep. 638), "a statute against law and reason, especially if a private [law] statute, is void." The case involved the College of Physicians having by parliamentary statute the authority to judge the fitness of practitioners to join. Coke threw out the law because it made the college judges in their own cause. The problem with this citation is that it had no firm basis in precedent, nor did it become a rule for English courts. Blackstone rejected the idea that the common law courts could decide whether acts of Parliament were void.

Hamilton's brief contained asides. These he labeled "Obj (objection)" and beneath each he cryptically responded. For example, "Obj: it has been said legislature may alter law of nations." He responded "Not true in theory." Then he added that if it were theoretically possible, the power would reside in the confederation Congress, not in the state legislature. A more important interior colloquy of this type followed: "Accession to [the] Confederation was act of legislature, Why may not another act [of the legislature] alter it?" In other words, by joining in the Confederation New York consented to Congress's power to impose treaty obligations on the state. The alternative, that the state might decide to depart the union, was a prospect that horrified Hamilton. But it was the very menace whose shadow fell over the case and all of the nation's politics in the confederation period. It had to be scotched immediately. Hamilton rushed to provide answers:

first, the "union preexisted" the state of New York, and second, "the act of accession not a law but a contract which one part[y] cannot release itself from."

Unfortunately, the first argument was circular, for it supposed a union bound the states together when in fact it was the signing of the Articles by the states that created the union. A committed nationalist might argue that the union was created by the adoption of independence, for that was when the term "United States of America" was coined and put into service by Congress. But as the weakness of the confederation demonstrated time and again, the union was a rope of sand. The second argument was flawed as well, for in contract law a party to a contract may seek its dissolution when the other party or parties do not perform their duties. This was precisely the basis for John C. Calhoun's theory of concurrent majorities in his 1828 *Exposition* and it was the constitutional rationale for states to secede from the Union in 1860–1861. Calhoun and the secessionists of 1860–1861 were wrong, but they were wrong because they applied their argument to the federal Constitution. A compact theory made more sense applied to the Articles of Confederation. In any case, there is no evidence that counsel for *Rutgers* wanted to make either of these arguments.

Hamilton's notes for the responses he planned to give to Benson's oral argument give us some idea of the give and take during the July 29 hearing in court. This document is labeled "Notes Upon Mr. Benson's argument, which as the de[fense] council [*sic*] were prevented from delivering are submitted." Hamilton evidently did not have the chance to respond in oral argument, and so wrote his responses. Hamilton's notes are the only direct evidence of Benson's contribution to the litigation. Benson proposed that the Trespass Act wholly controlled the case, and no reference to the law of nations or the Peace Treaty of 1783 or examples from other times and places applied. The State of New York was sovereign, and its positive law, not treaties, or treatises or British common law doctrines should govern the outcome. What was more, again anticipating the defense (because both Lawrence and Benson had undoubtedly read *Phocion* and knew Hamilton would use its arguments in the Mayor's Court), Benson continued that the treaty provisions, no matter how twisted and tugged at, said nothing contrary to or barring the operation of the Trespass Act. Having thrown the law of nations out the front door, lest anyone try to sneak it in the back door Benson added that the war was an unjust one and a party waging an unjust war cannot sustain any gain from it or protect the gains of any who served it. The war was not a "solemn" one waged under the laws of war, and so these did not apply to Waddington.

Like Mentor, Benson had little desire to engage in a contest of authorities or travel the byways of the law of war with Hamilton. He tried to persuade the court against such a course. He wanted to confine the argument to "the consideration of the act." Were he successful, all of Hamilton's erudition would have been irrelevant. Hamilton knew that, and wanted to argue that one could not interpret the statute on its face. One had to look at the principles that governed the interpretation of statutes. Benson next submitted that one could not regard the law of war as a fixed body of rules, a code, when it changed constantly. Here again, Benson rejected theory in favor of practice. Given the chance, Hamilton would have replied that the "present state of the laws of nations" gave rise to the principles he explored. The two men agreed that the court acted within its charge in interpreting the Trespass Act but disagreed about what should govern that interpretation. How frustrated Hamilton must have been that the court did not allow him to make these rejoinders in court. And with that, the case was submitted to the bench.

CHAPTER FOUR

"A Cause of National Significance"

On June 29, oral argument in *Rutgers v. Waddington* began and ended, and counsel deposited written briefs with the court. Duane recognized from the start how important the case, hence his opinion, would be. He might have rested with the decision on the case that he rendered on August 17. He might have authored a very short opinion and delivered it then. He did neither. Instead, he agonized over what to say and how to say it. As he wrote to the aldermen on August 14, nearly a month and half after counsel and parties left his presence, "a number of days have already been devoted by myself, and by the recorder [Varick] . . . in considering the authorities and argument offered by the counsel on both sides . . . and [we] hope to be able to form an opinion thereon by the sitting of the court which will take place on Tuesday next." Although Duane said that he was working with Varick, there is no evidence in the Varick or the Duane papers that he added anything to the opinion. Duane had not called the aldermen together in conference to hash out an opinion, "till we should have done with [the draft]." He added that if any of the aldermen wanted to give the draft opinion a once-over, the law books and copies of the briefs were available at his office. None of the aldermen seem to have taken advantage of this offer, as Duane probably expected.

On August 17, he read his decision in court. He delivered his opinion ten days later, on August 27. There were two parts to the decision and two to the opinion. The two pieces of the decision interlocked as Duane split the difference in the back rent owed according to the two principles of the law of war he applied. From 1778 to 1780, the merchants Waddington and Pierrepont occupied the premises on assignment from a civilian officer of the occupation. They were thus not acting under direct military orders. For that period of time, he

judged, they owed back rent. From 1780 to 1783, when their continued occupation was directed by a serving military officer, and they
paid £150 yearly as rent to the military authorities, they were not
liable for back rent. He promised to empanel a jury to determine the
exact amount owed. As the occupation occurred before the act was
passed, it did not figure in Duane's decision, even though the legislature regarded it as a remedial act that applied to the wartime years.

————

In a common law system, precedent—the opinion of courts on a
prior case on point—has great weight. If the precedent came from an
appellate court in the same jurisdiction as faced the present case, that
precedent might be compelling. If it came from an appellate court in
another jurisdiction, for example another state's supreme court, the
precedent might be persuasive, but the present court did not have to
follow it. Duane might have known about comparable issues facing
a handful of state courts prior to *Rutgers*. None of these precedents
would have dictated his own opinion, however. What is more, none
of them was reported at the time as an example of judicial review. Of
course, historians know about all of them, an example of the judicial
omniscience that sometimes attributes to contemporary jurists what
later scholars have found. In any case, a few episodes of the *Rutgers*
type did precede that case.

In 1780, a New Jersey supreme court reputedly overturned a lower
court's ruling in a case of the seizure of Loyalist property because the
lower court jury, as provided by the confiscation statute, was composed of only six men, instead of the twelve implied by the state constitution's provision "that the inestimable right of trial by jury shall
remain confirmed." The decision was given orally and there existed
no written record of it. The case, *Holmes v. Watson*, was cited in an
1802 New Jersey case and elevated as an example of judicial review by
a scholar nearly 100 years later. The case was not precisely on point,
however, because the court did not claim the authority to overturn
a state law; it merely found for the appellant on grounds that there
should have been twelve jurors rather than six.

The Virginia "Prisoners' Case" (*Commonwealth v. Caton* [1782])
was fully argued before the Virginia Court of Appeals and it centered

on a conflict between the state constitution and an act of the state House of Delegates. Three Loyalists convicted in a lower court of waging war against the state argued that their House of Delegates pardon was sufficient to overcome their conviction. The state constitution of 1776 had given the lower house this power. A year later the legislature passed a law requiring both houses to concur in any such pardon. The three men carried out their illegal acts, were captured, and convicted under the 1777 statute, then pardoned by the lower house. Edmund Pendleton, the presiding judge, asked counsel and members of the bar present in the court whether a court of law could find an act of the legislature violated the constitution, and in consequence could declare the act void. Representing the state, Attorney General Edmund Randolph conceded that the court could void the statute if it found a violation of the constitution (though he thought this time it did not). Counsel for the three prisoners at the bar argued that the statute did violate the constitution. St. George Tucker, a much-respected lawyer, legal scholar, and future state supreme court judge, agreed with Randolph that statutes contradicting the constitution must be void. On the bench, Chancellor George Wythe, the foremost teacher of law in the state (he tutored Thomas Jefferson and John Marshall), went further than Tucker. Statutes that violated the constitution were void from the start, and courts must declare them so.

While *Holmes* was not on point for *Rutgers*, *Caton* was, and it would have deprived *Rutgers* of pride of place as the first case of judicial review in the new nation, had Daniel Call, the Virginia lawyer who collected and published the early state cases a generation after they were decided, recorded the colloquy above. But Call was not present at the time "The Prisoners' Case" was argued and did not include the oral exchange over judicial review in his report of *Commonwealth v. Caton*. Instead, the only report of Randolph's, Tucker's, and Wythe's comments appears in private correspondence between Randolph and James Madison. While the correspondence proved that the issue was a real one for contemporaries, it cannot stand as the case of first instance of judicial review. It was not widely disseminated nor did the outcome of the case turn on it. Instead, in Calls' *Reports*, Wythe pronounced the opinion of the court: "The sole enquiry therefore is, whether the pardon be valid? If we consider the genius of our institutions, it is clear, that the pretensions of the house of delegates cannot be sustained. For, throughout the whole structure of the government, concurrence of the several branches of each department is required to give effect to its operations." In short, Wythe agreed with Randolph's interpretation of the law, without reference to judicial review. Edmund Pendleton's concurring opinion adopted a similar stance.

> But how far this court, in whom the judiciary powers may in some sort be said to be concentrated, shall have power to declare the nullity of a law passed in its forms by the legislative power, without exercising the power of that branch, contrary to the plain terms of that constitution, is indeed a deep, important, and I will add, a tremendous question, the decision of which might involve consequences to which gentlemen may not have extended their ideas. I am happy in being of opinion there is no occasion to consider it upon this occasion.

The account of the prisoners may have caused a commotion at the time in Williamsburg, but there is no evidence whatsoever that Hamilton and Duane were aware of it. Because the discussion of judicial review was never published, Duane and Hamilton may have thought that they were navigating uncharted waters. Indeed, not only were provisions for judicial review absent from state constitutions, the very structure of state government in 1784 seemed to weight the scales against the courts striking down an act or a portion of an act of the legislature. The Virginia Constitution of 1776 to which counsel for the three prisoners appealed contained the provision, "All power of suspending laws, or the execution of laws, by any authority, without consent of the representatives of the people, is injurious to their rights, and ought not to be exercised." The Massachusetts Constitution made this point explicitly: "The judicial shall never exercise the legislative and executive powers, or either of them." In New York, the state constitution authorized the Council of Revision to stay the passage of laws its members felt violated the constitution. On the council sat the state's chief justice and its chancellor. But the assembly could override the stay. The governor could refuse to sign a law, but again his refusal could be overridden by the legislature. In short, the authority for the new republican states' law was the legislature.

Hence Hamilton needed the three-step incorporation argument he deployed in *Rutgers*: military necessity was part of the laws of war, the laws of war were part of the law of nations, and the law of nations was part of the common law adopted by the state constitution. That argument involved a lot of fancy stepping. Duane's task was as difficult, but different from Hamilton's. As an advocate, Hamilton had license to rummage through treatises on the law of war and the law of nations to make the best case for his client that he could. Duane was bound by a stricter, judicial, canon. He and his fellow judges had a duty to stay within the boundaries of settled law. He was not as free as Hamilton to range through foreign authorities or make connections between disparate bodies of law.

———

Duane's opinion opened with a statement of the importance of the case and alerted readers that he would venture into all of the arcane legal issues Hamilton visited. "We have gone further perhaps into many important subjects which have been brought into view by this controversy than was strictly necessary." Rather than simply say that the Trespass Act was passed after the events at issue occurred, and so was an ex post facto measure barred by the common law, or it was passed after the provisions of the treaty were known, and hence was an attempt to preemptively avoid obeying the treaty, he explored the larger issues of state sovereignty. Nearly all of the opinion related to the treaty question, the powers of Congress, the nature of the Union, and "a sense of national obligation." Duane had concluded that only an opinion fully addressing all of Hamilton's points would "ease the mind of a multitude of suitors whose causes are depending here under this statute." Given this purpose, it was not surprising that Duane's opinion was framed by Hamilton's brief. Not that Duane was willing to be seen as Hamilton's tool—periodically Duane praised "the attorney general's" [Benson] contributions to the argument. Duane tried, albeit in what seems at this distance to be a half-hearted way, to give space and weight to the plaintiff's case.

One further point about procedure cannot be ignored because it hovered in the background of the entire proceeding. As Duane noted, he was concerned that a magistrate's court like the Mayor's Court found on its docket a case of such importance. Magistrates courts did not, as a rule, issue opinions, one reason why Duane severed the decision (the ordinary work product of a magistrates' court) from the opinion. In writing an opinion of any length, Duane was taking on himself and his bench the role of an appeals court like the New York Supreme Court, or the State Court for the Trial of Impeachments and for the Correction of Errors. Of necessity, every common law court has to decide if a statute or statutes on which parties rely actually apply, but the interpretation of the meaning of the statute and the intent of the legislature was a task of some magnitude not entered into lightly by a municipal court.

Duane conceded at the outset that the case had excited great attention both domestically and in Britain because it would define the powers and the limitations on the powers of the states of the new republic. This, in turn, would influence the way in which foreign powers and their citizens viewed the new nation's prospects. For this reason, the opinion was almost as much a diplomatic document as a domestic legal one.

Duane's opinion had two parts not nearly as well delineated as the parts of his decision. One part of the opinion regarded the legal rules under which the back rent was due in time of war. Reading it one can almost sense Hamilton's hand guiding Duane's pen. The second part of the opinion went far beyond rent to examine the public policy issues that Hamilton had raised.

In the first part of the opinion, Duane found the plaintiff's claim within the scope of the act. Was the defendant "intended" to be included in the Trespass Act? Yes. The act was a "remedial" one, designed to restore to the claimant lost revenues. He brushed away the issue of whether the act was an ex post facto law. He assumed that the act was to be interpreted equitably, in short, fairly to all parties. At this point in the opinion Duane seemed to be giving to both sides the victory, or at least going back and forth between them. He continued in this vein: If the merchants had come to the city to benefit from the distress of its exiled property owners, to further their private interests and "enrich themselves by its spoils," then they were liable to the act's penalties. If they were in the power of the British occupiers, and obeyed their commands, then they had a defense against the rigors of the act. In full cry now, Duane wondered why the merchants "even wish to be exempted [from paying rent] at the expense of a widow, driven into exile by the dread of a siege?" This was the revolutionary politician speaking—for after all, who could blame the poor widow deprived of her valuable property in her declining years. (The fact that Rutgers was anything but poor did not matter.) His conclusion: the occupation was related to the war.

Following Hamilton, Duane asserted that the New York constitution incorporated the law of nations. "By our excellent constitution, the common law is declared to be part of the law of the land, and the [law of nations] is a branch of the common law." But Hamilton wanted the law of nations to be an enforceable part of the constitution, controlling the acts of the legislature. Correctly reading Blackstone where Hamilton had not, Duane found the strictures of the law of nations a moral rather than a controlling element of the state law. Then, again following Hamilton, Duane suggested that no state could unilaterally nullify a provision of the treaty ending the war, for that would be "contrary to the very nature of the confederacy," but Duane did not take the next step and conclude that Congress could in any way impose its will on the state.

What was left? Duane could not conceive that the legislature would punish those who obeyed the occupying power. But "other considerations" must "have their weight." The war did not "bar" the suit. As illuminating as Hamilton's lessons in the "interesting science" of the law of nations might be, it did not all apply to the new American states. Duane agreed with Benson: the law of nations only bound sovereign states insofar as they adopted those laws. What was more, insofar as the various sources of international law that Hamilton had cited could be reconciled (for often they disagreed), it was clear that only the direct command of the British military authority could relieve Waddington of the obligation to pay rent for the property from which he profited. This portion of the opinion seemed to bow to Benson's argument, not Hamilton's.

Duane elided discussion of the great irony of the revolutionary settlements of the states. The powers in question were legislative acts.

Despite resisting parliamentary claims of absolute supremacy, the Revolutionaries made their own state legislatures far more powerful than the other branches of government, particularly the state courts. To be sure, New York's constitution, like that of Massachusetts and others, created a system of checks and balances preventing any one branch from accumulating all power. But the Trespass Act had passed the legislature, been signed by the governor, and was already upheld in other court cases. Thus, to disavow the Trespass Act, for whatever reason, was to call into question the sovereignty of the people in their representative assemblies. Duane thus insisted, indeed protested too much, that the supremacy of the legislature must be conceded by all.

But Duane's next passages proved Benson's victory was short-lived. One could interpret the meaning of the Trespass Act—that, after all, is what judges did in the common law system: they determined legislative intent. Duane suggested that the court was free to "expound the statute by equity." Given that the Mayor's Court did not use equitable procedure and was not a court of equity, the phrasing here seems to make little sense. Perhaps the term was used loosely, suggesting that the court should try to be fair to both sides. The decision on the 17th had done pretty much that. One might argue that the judges of the Mayor's Court had a duty to their office, the state, and the parties before them to examine whether a statute on which a party relied was in fact applicable. There is a better explanation of the equity of the statute to which we will come shortly.

Everyone in the courtroom knew what the letter of the law was—the Trespass Act was remedial legislation to restore to owners of property in the city all that they had lost by reason of the British occupation. Duane's listeners also knew the intent of the legislature. The act was part of a code of legal impositions on the Loyalists. But Duane, with feigned astonishment, could not believe that the Trespass Act intended to violate the law of nations. All relations among nations would be thrown into chaos, a void without reason or law, were the Trespass Act so read. So it must be read to incorporate the basic ideas of the law of nations.

What then to do with the very explicit clause of the Trespass Act that forbade a defense based on military orders? Duane constructed the meaning of the act backwards—the clause could not include "occupation" when the British commander imposed the occupation on his agents. To read the clause in this manner would mean that Rutgers had legitimate claims against General Guy Carleton, the last British commander in chief. That surely was an absurdity. There must be some wiggle room in the law to allow occupiers to plead military necessity in their own defense.

Duane's opinion did not spell out the amount of damages that would equal back rent. Lawrence's original pleading included the amount that Rutgers wanted. When the decision came down, on August 17, Duane had ordered a jury empanelled, and on September 2, it reported its finding. Rutgers was due £791 and some change (a little under $114,000 in 2014 U.S. dollars). On the next meeting of the Mayor's Court, on September 7, Duane ordered the defendants to pay this sum. An award less than one-tenth of the damages Elizabeth Rutgers sought was unacceptable to her, and on October 12, Lawrence appeared in court with a writ of error. Duane ordered that it be forwarded to the supreme court of the state. There is some evidence by way of Hamilton's recollection in a letter to Thomas Jefferson dated April 19, 1792, that he also filed a writ of error seeking to overturn the entire judgment against his clients. For almost a year, the writs waited in the queue on the desk of the clerk of the state supreme court. Then, in July 1785, the parties compromised. The exact sum remains unknown, but as the British commander had only ordered Waddington to pay £150 rent a year, a judgment of five times as much for only three years would seem much less burdensome than the £8000 Rutgers wanted.

———

Duane accomplished a great feat in very subtle steps of expanding the role for judges in the post-revolutionary world. In a system of parliamentary imperial supremacy, when colonial courts were merely inferior tribunals whose every decision had, in theory, no precedential weight, American colonial courts could hardly exercise judicial review. Colonial courts could and did act in ways contrary to royal instructions and tortured parliamentary acts all out of shape. But the introduction of a system of checks and balances in new states' governments changed the necessity for such subterfuges and evasions. Checks and balances gave courts not only the means to defend themselves against the incursions of the other branches of republican state government, it afforded courts the opportunity to interpret the meaning and application of legislation. Whether this extended to the power to strike down legislation as unconstitutional—to exercise what was later called "judicial review"—was at least in part the issue in *Rutgers.*

For this achievement, Hamilton has received credit that rightfully belongs to Duane. Counsel can only ask a court to declare a piece of legislation unconstitutional. Equally uncharitably, later commentators have found Duane's opinion wordy and blurry, an awkward exercise of legal gymnastics. Such judgments underestimate the obstacles he faced in getting where he wanted to go and his cleverness in surmounting them. Three of these obstacles stood in the path to overcome the clause of the Trespass Act barring the military necessity defense. Only by rising above these obstacles could he coherently and effectively nullify the objectionable portion of the legislation.

To surmount the first of the obstacles, Duane had to assert or assume that the state constitution controlled legislation, that is, that the New York constitution was the fundamental law against which legislation had to be measured. This was a novel argument for an Anglo-American jurist, because after the "Glorious Revolution" of 1689 Parliament was supreme. Its legislation was the constitution and it could say what that legislation meant. Although some historians have argued along lines laid down by the revolutionary lawyers that there was an English constitution controlling Parliament, that is a minority view. By contrast with English public law, the new state constitutions were the foundations on which the will of the people rested. The writing of constitutions preceded and empowered government and had to be ratified to go into force. The very core of revolutionary self-government was that the people were sovereign. Thus in theory portions or the whole of acts of legislatures could be compared with the constitution and found to violate it and thereby voided.

But who was to do this? Duane had to prove that courts were proper, legitimate institutions to weigh the constitutionality of legislation, the second obstacle. Precedent for this lay not in colonial courts' powers, but in the revolutionary doctrine of separation of powers. Colonial courts could not overturn colonial legislation. Should a litigant seek this kind of relief, appeal was to be made to the King's Privy Council or his courts. On a number of occasions, for example a question arising about Connecticut inheritance statutes, the Privy Council did review the constitutionality of colonial laws. With the ties to Britain cut and the new state of New York constitution delineating the powers of the various branches of government, something like the role of the Privy Council was assigned to the Council of Revision. But the Council of Revision could not overturn state legislation.

Where then lay succor for those litigants who claimed that an act of the legislature violated the state constitution? The answer was the courts. The separation of powers of the branches of government spelled out in the constitution would be effectuated by the operation of each branch through "checks and balances." Each branch could check and balance the others. In revolutionary treatises like John Adams's *Thoughts on Government* (1776), the independence of the judicial branch was tied to its capacity to review legislation. Written to influence the shaping of a new constitution for Massachusetts, the tract asked, rhetorically, "As good government is an empire of laws, how shall your laws be made?" Adams hated multiple office holding and advised that no official should be allowed to hold more than one. According to Adams, separation of powers would safeguard the republic from corruption by reserving the making of the laws to the legislature, execution of the laws to the executive, and adjudication of disputes to the courts. The legislature was no longer to act as a court, nor the governor to sit as a judge.

Adams insisted that the independence of the judiciary in the state was essential to prevent its capture by the legislature or its domination by the executive. "The dignity and stability of government in all its branches, the morals of the people, and every blessing of society depend so much upon an upright and skillful administration of justice that the judicial power ought to be distinct from both the legislative and executive, and independent upon both, that so it may be a check upon both, as both should be checks upon that."

Adams's formulation of the idea of separation of powers became a hallmark of revolutionary constitutionalism. In the new republican regime, it took the courts out of the grasp (if not the reach) of the elective executive and legislative offices, away from the influence of the mob, the influence peddlers, and the potential tyrant—almost. Thomas Jefferson, a lawyer with an extensive practice in his state's courts, still worried that the legislature of Virginia could "decide rights which should have been left to the judiciary."

It was the independence of the judiciary from the legislative branch that made review of legislation in the courts possible. Safeguarded from legislators' retaliation by this tool, courts could check legislatures whose temporary majority or temporary insanity championed laws violating the constitution even as Duane conceded that "the supremacy of the legislature need not be called into question." The courts did not represent the sovereignty of the people as directly as the legislatures, but in separation of powers theory courts were part of the republican regime. Whether Duane, or Duane's court, was competent to exercise this power was another matter—and the grounds for clamor against the decision in the lower house and out of doors.

The final obstacle Duane had to surmount was to establish that the Trespass Act's barring of the military necessity defense violated the state constitution. He recognized that the constitution explicitly incorporated such of the common law as was practiced in 1775. He conceded that the common law included the law of nations. But the very clause that incorporated the common law continued that incorporation was controlled by a qualifying provision: "subject to such alterations and provisions as the legislature of this State shall, from time to time, make concerning the same."

Here is where Duane's political delicacy came into play. Instead of announcing that the offending clause of the Trespass Act violated the state constitution, Duane offered that it could not have been the intent of the legislature to violate the constitution, hence they had not. Logically, then, he must read the act as allowing the defense of military necessity in certain cases. He did not assert the doctrine of judicial review. He did not exercise judicial review explicitly. He merely put himself in the minds of the legislators and found it impossible that they could have meant to violate the constitution. This given, any part of the Trespass Act that violated the common law doctrines of military necessity must have allowed for the *Rutgers* exception.

Duane did not expound on the fact that *Rutgers* was a case in which the legislature had proscribed a particular defense in certain types of lawsuits. As such, it directly impinged on what remedies a court might offer parties. It is because of this procedural question that the reference to the "equity" of the statute in the opinion makes sense. An inferior court was not a tribunal in which one expected the parsing of legislative provisions—except when they directly affected the operation of that very court. Equity in this context was not being fair to the parties standing before the court, it was fairness to the court itself. Although Duane did not dwell on this aspect of the Trespass Act, its impact on court proceedings gave Duane's opinion a weight it might not otherwise have had.

This last point requires further exploration. Constitutional provisions establishing state courts notwithstanding, state statutes routinely defined process in bringing a suit, channeling the types of pleading allowed, determining who could do the pleading, and filling out areas of jurisdiction, which tersely composed constitutions elided. Both the constitution and the acts of the legislature were examples of public law. Public law was general and prospective, applying to the people as a whole. Public law defined relations between the government and the populace. Legislation like the Trespass Act lay on the boundary between public and private law. Private law looked back to past wrongs, including suits by an individual or group in the private sector against other private individuals or groups. Providing an action for damages for back rent during the war straddled that boundary. It allowed a private claim for an act carried out in the public arena according to the orders of a military government. Duane's opinion concluded that the legislature could not have intended to cross this boundary. In effect, he said that the military necessity defense was a matter of public policy, not subject to review in a private law action.

In writing that he was looking to legislative intent, Duane was engaging in an activity very different from the interpretation of legislature intent today. Duane knew very well what the intent of the legislature was. He did not have to sift through records of the debates over the act as a modern judge would have to do. He knew that the statute was part of the Loyalist Code meant to punish those who remained loyal to the crown. His reading of the statute against that purpose was not the act of a dutiful judge. Nor did it have much in the way of precedent.

The first full-blown treatment of legislative intent came many years after *Rutgers*. Francis Lieber's 1838 treatise on statutory interpretation, *Legal and Political Hermeneutics, or Principles of Interpretation and Construction in Law and Politics*, was the first of the modern tracts on the subject. Lieber was born in Germany and educated in its universities in mathematics. A republican advocate in a monarchical system, he found a more receptive intellectual home in Boston, where he established himself as an educator, and later in Columbia, South Carolina, where he taught history and philosophy. In 1856 he returned to the North and joined the faculty at Columbia University. During and after the war he served the federal government in a variety of capacities.

In his essay on interpretation of statutes, he argued that all speech and writings only gave their full meaning after interpretation by the appropriate audience. "Interpretation of some sort or other is always requisite." In that effort, he offered a compendium of "true and safe principles of interpretation." He conceded that English and American authorities too often criticized courts for acting as legislatures, supplanting legislative intent with the judge's own, but "the freer the country the more necessary becomes interpretation." According to Lieber (or at least the interpretation of Lieber's text given here), judges like Duane were "constructing" the meaning of the law by "drawing" from the text certain conclusions "respecting subjects that lie beyond the direct expression of the text . . . causing the text to agree and harmonize with the demands of superior authority." Without construction, the inferior text, the statute, would "produce the very opposite of what it was purposed to effect."

It is anachronistic to read Lieber back into Duane, but Duane said exactly what Lieber would later say. If one read the Trespass Act to bar the defense of military necessity, it would violate the superior principle that the state constitution had received the law of war by its incorporation of common law. If the legislature insisted on this interpretation of its own handiwork, the statute would work the very harm—unfair dispossession of property—that it was intended to remedy. Duane refused to regard the statute as a simple act of revenge. Had he done so, it would not have mattered whether it violated the laws of war or the state constitution. But by constructing its meaning in the fashion that Lieber later described, Duane elevated the legislature's intent from exacting revenge to acting in the public weal. That is, Duane read the statute to promote the good of all the people of the state, the "true spirit" according to Lieber, of all public law.

In one recent and authoritative study of colonial law, William Nelson insisted that the determinations of courts were far more important than the output of colonial legislatures. This was patently untrue for the colonial period, as legislation affected everyone in the jurisdiction but court decisions affected only those who sued or were sued, and because colonial courts' decisions were not precedent for later colonial cases. But *Rutgers v. Waddington*, in the context of the emerging doctrine of separation of powers and the practice of checks and balances in republican constitutions, signaled the end of the inferiority of courts.

——————

It will occur to students of modern courts that judges and advocates sometimes converse about a case in chambers or out of doors. Duane and Hamilton were neighbors in New York City, both were members of Trinity Church, and both spent a lot of time in and around City Hall. Was there communication between the two men of an untoward sort during the time that Duane was writing his opinion? Had Hamilton anything more to do with Duane's opinion than was proper for counsel and judge in ongoing litigation, something beyond submitting appropriate and respectful pleadings at appropriate times, not trying the court's patience, and preparing and submitting a written brief to accompany oral argument. As the foremost scholarly authority on the Mayor's Court, Richard B. Morris, noted many years ago, after the war the Mayor's Court opened its doors to many more lawyers than the small coterie that had practiced in the prewar court. Hamilton had only practiced for two years. Duane was new to his job on the bench, having just become mayor. It would not have been unthinkable for the two men, who lived and worked in such close proximity, to have shared their thinking.

What is more, the relationship between the two men preceded the filing of *Rutgers* and was not simply a social one. Hamilton's correspondence with Duane was of a deeply political cast and it foreordained what may be called their collaboration on *Rutgers*. The Hamilton who lectured, for want of a better word, Duane on the laws of war and the law of nations in *Rutgers* was also the Hamilton who courted Duane with praise and humility before *Rutgers*. Duane was not oblivious or indifferent to Hamilton's efforts. On October 18, 1780, Duane wrote to Hamilton, "Be assured, My Dear Sir, the marks of your regard give me a sincere pleasure, and I shall be always happy to cultivate it, and to give you proofs of my affectionate attachment." At Washington's side during most of the fighting, Hamilton kept Duane apprised of military affairs. Duane kept Hamilton up to date on New York events. When Hamilton informed Duane that he was preparing for the bar, on May 5, 1782, Duane generously and genuinely replied: "I am much pleased to find you have set yourself seriously to the study of the law. You are welcome to the use of any of my books." Hamilton and Duane subsequently faced one another in their capacities of attorneys in 1783, but there was no rivalry, as with Burr.

Hamilton was not entirely satisfied with Duane's opinion, though he could hardly have asked for better. In the Hamilton papers there is a final brief, undated and untitled. A clue to its purpose lay in its first paragraph: "Question now is whether a judgment already given in an inferior court consonant with our best interests shall be reversed in a superior court." Plainly, Hamilton thought he had won what he could for his client, but in this brief Hamilton had put his finger on the issue that Duane evaded—whether an inferior court—the Mayor's Court—could make law. From this and other internal evidence the document must have been prepared after Duane had rendered his opinion and Lawrence had brought his writ of error to the court. The appeal was never heard, however. In any case, there was little new in the brief. It did feature a great deal from Emmerich de Vattel, Hamilton now using it rather than Blackstone as his bible.

Vattel was the most generous law of nations theorist when it came to forgiving one's enemies in times of civil insurrection. The Swiss diplomat and philosopher's commentaries were widely read and highly regarded. His work was based on the long history of European diplomatic relations, Roman law, and other sources. Vattel had no formal weight in any Anglo-American jurisdiction. His commentaries were not law and no one had to obey his admonitions. But for Hamilton, citation of Vattel was not just window dressing, a show of learning that transcended the provincialism of Lawrence's pleading. Vattel represented the wider world of natural law, a higher standard of legal ideology than simple state sovereignty. On this somewhat slender line of reasoning, from the common law incorporated in the state constitution to the law of nations incorporated in the common law, to Vattel's views of the treatment of losers in civil wars, Hamilton intended to rest his argument in the supreme court. How much of this natural law would make its way into the jurisprudence of American courts was an open question then, and remains so to this day.

Perhaps it is time to ask seriously whether Hamilton knew very much about natural law, and, even more important for an assessment of his thinking, how much he really cared about it. Modern legal scholars, including students of Hamilton's jurisprudential ideas, know a great deal more than he did—or could for that matter—about natural law. He cited Blackstone and Vattel, but even the most modest modern law library will have Grotius, Pufendorf, and other sources on its shelves along with a myriad of nineteenth- and twentieth century tracts. His practice manual did not include practice of natural law, because there was no actual practice of it. Nor could one practice the law of nations or the laws of war, for that matter. Blackstone was not really on point for him and Vattel was relatively new on the scene.

The revolutionary generation had explored the concept of natural rights in the course of disputing the absolute sovereignty of Parliament. They argued that parliamentary enactments could not violate the natural rights of all men, a stance enshrined in Thomas Jefferson's immortal declamation of the right to life, liberty, and the pursuit of happiness. But courts were not the protectors of these inalienable rights. As Jefferson continued in the Declaration of Independence, the king was censurable for "he has made Judges dependent on his

Will alone, for the tenure of their offices, and the amount and payment of their salaries." One has to look very hard indeed to find a revolutionary who extolled courts as the first line of defense of the rights of the people. Instead, the revolutionary embodiment of this natural law was the sovereignty of the people as expressed in their state constitutions and as put in practice by their elected legislatures.

But both of these seemed unlikely places to find grounds for the appeal of Waddington's case. The law of nations was implicitly received in the New York State constitution (as part of the common law) with a caveat, "subject to such alterations and provisions as the legislature of this State shall, from time to time, make concerning the same." The Trespass Act, passed after the preliminaries of the treaty were widely circulated and certainly known to the legislators, was one such alteration—even if the treaty had explicitly protected Loyalists and sojourning English merchants in the City, which it did not. But Hamilton was nothing if not ingenious.

Hamilton recognized the relationship between the revolutionary rhetoric of natural law and the sovereignty of the people but he placed that sovereignty not in the state legislature or the state constitution. Instead, he noted in the appellate brief that "Congress then had complete sovereignty." Hamilton emphasized this with three exclamation points. This comment applied to the treaty obligations, and in context meant that any claim New York had to abrogate or modify the terms of the treaty bowed to Congress's authority. Hamilton continued, "The first act of our government adopts it as fundament law . . . these reflections teach us to respect the sovereignty of the union and to consider its constitution powers as not controllable by any state."

Whatever the validity of Hamilton's short passage as a matter of law, it implied a great deal about his notion of the relationship between the states and the confederation, hinting that the Articles of Confederation should be viewed as a federal system. The problem with this argument was that the Articles of Confederation gave to the Congress exclusive authority to conclude treaties, but they did not provide a mechanism for enforcing the terms of the treaty on the sovereign states. Even if Hamilton believed in the concept of natural law, and knew enough about it to make a case for its application, that argument would not have been conclusive.

Indeed, a review of the history, text, and practice of Congress under the Articles of Confederation shows that Hamilton's reading of the document was aspirational rather than accurate. Article II of the Articles of Confederation confirmed that "Each state retains its sovereignty, freedom, and independence, and every power, jurisdiction, and right, which is not by this Confederation expressly delegated to the United States, in Congress assembled." The Congress, representing the confederation of the states, had exclusive control over the making of war and the concluding of peace, but nothing was said about treaties usurping the sovereignty of states or making the confederation itself into a supreme sovereign. There was no implied powers provision in the Articles, allowing the Congress an expansive reading of the text. The Articles declared themselves, and the union they defined, as perpetual, but without the power to tax, without courts, without the power to compel states or the citizens of states to obey its commands, the confederation could hardly be called a sovereign government.

Hamilton knew all this from his service in Congress. He kept current on the state of affairs in the country in 1784. That he argued for a much stronger central government was not a matter of restating the law. It was an aspiration not shared by everyone. According to one broadside that appeared soon after *Rutgers* was decided, the meaning of the Trespass Law "was expressed in plain and unequivocal language" understood by "all the gentlemen of the law" until "the case of Rutgers and Waddington was agitated . . . inventing distinctions where there was no difference and introducing matter which the [trespass] law prohibited." The author of the blast against Duane and the decision had no doubt of the "evils which will result" from the decision, though he declined to name them. Better to appeal the case to the state supreme court, though in the end counsel for *Rutgers* did not follow that suggestion.

———

Members of the state assembly took the *Rutgers* opinion and the outcome of the case not as a compromise nor a necessary step toward reconciliation with former Loyalists or future citizens from Britain, but as an affront to the sovereignty of the state and the honor of the drafters of the Trespass Act. On October 27, 1784, William Harper of Montgomery County offered a resolution condemning Duane's opinion. Tryon County (the name was changed in 1784 to Montgomery, in part to honor the heroism of General Richard Montgomery in the invasion of Canada, in part to wipe away the memory of royal Governor William Tryon) was a cockpit of the Revolution, the Mohawk Valley lying in the pathway of invasion from Canada. The Patriots had scourged the land of Loyalists in 1776, including Mohawk leader Joseph Brant, but the fighting had not ended there until 1782. Harper was one of the first members of the county committee of safety, a member of the provincial congress and the assembly, and a leader of the state militia. His escape from Mohawk and Loyalist captors in 1780 became part of the lore of the Mohawk Valley in the war.

Harper's resolution, included verbatim in the journal of assembly, pleaded that

> whereas, at a later trial before the mayor's court, in the city and county of New York, in a suit commenced by Rutgers against Waddington, on the act for granting a more effectual relief, in cases of certain trespasses, in the judgment of the same court, or the said trial, it was declared, that such part of the act as specially provides that no defendant shall be admitted to plead, in justification any military order or command whatsoever . . . was incompatible with the law of nations . . . resolved, that the adjudication aforesaid, in its tendency, is subversive of all law and good order, and leads directly to anarchy and confusion . . . in a direct violation of a plain and known law of the state.

With it as precedent, any court might dispense with any of the acts of the legislature, "and legislatures become useless." The resolution then recommended to the council of appointments that it convey the assembly's feeling to the members of the Mayor's Court. But the resolution, after debate, was postponed. The members of the Mayor's Court were men of high stature and great repute, and the resolution accused them of serious offenses.

Defenders of the legislature's Loyalist Code did not confine themselves to resolutions. They took the matter to the public. On November 4, 1784, an open letter from leading merchant Melancton

Smith, who had relocated from Long Island to New York City, and eight others accused the Mayor's Court of "setting aside" the will of the people and the letter of the law. The letter reminded readers that the legislative authority must be supreme if the objectives of the Revolution were to be met, and that authority must include the interpretation of the legislature's own intent. Like Harper's resolution, nothing came of the letter.

Duane remained proud of his opinion, and of its "enlarged and liberal principles," as he wrote to George Washington on December 16, 1784. He was surprised and stung by the "censure" in the newspaper. In an unusual step, he caused his opinion to be published "to answer some beneficial purposes and would at least serve to prevent misapprehension," at the "request of several citizens."

If the members of the court were safe from the censure of the legislature and the calumny of the public prints, Duane still found himself and his opinion in *Rutgers* swimming against the tide of post-revolutionary radicalism in New York. A core of reformers in the legislature, aided and abetted by Governor Clinton, had swept away entail and primogeniture (the foundations in estate law of the great patroonships), and pushed hard against the constitution's conservative provisions for voting and holding office. Some of the reformers even pressed for the end of chattel slavery in the state. Sympathetic to the more conservative aspects of this program (for example the gradual end to slavery) but opposed to the more democratic portions of the radical agenda, Hamilton and others struggled to gain control of the state government. Only the radicals' tendency to splinter and quarrel prevented a genuine political upheaval in the years after the war. In the meantime, Duane's opinion went out into the world, its legacy reaching into the most significant currents of opinion in the last days of the confederation and the first days of the federal union.

Duane was circumspect in his conduct and cautious in his jurisprudence, but Hamilton was not. Never one to let the opposition have the last word, as he was preparing to leave the Albany session of the state legislature on April 17, 1787, to journey to the Philadelphia constitutional convention, he proposed that the legislature declare void all laws in contravention of the Peace Treaty of 1783. In the course of his remarks, Hamilton told his fellow assemblymen,

"It had been said that the judges would have too much power; this was misapprehended. He stated the powers of the judges with great clearness and precision. He insisted that their powers would be the same, whether this law was passed or not. For, that as all treaties were known by the constitution as the laws of the land, so must the judges act on the same, any law to the contrary notwithstanding."

CHAPTER FIVE

The Many Legacies of *Rutgers*

On its face, *Rutgers v. Waddington* concerned three British merchants and a Patriot family. But Duane's opinion went far beyond the claims and counterclaims of the parties. In the course of rescuing the British merchants from what in other judicial hands might have been total defeat, Duane's opinion broadened the scope of the case from a New York State civil suit under a state law to a defense of the contributions of former Loyalists to the new nation, a referendum on the treaty powers of Congress, and an essay on the laws of war. *Rutgers* was a closely watched case and the opinion widely read. Thus its legacy extended to all of these subjects—the resuscitation of New York City; an evolving conception of federalism; and what was soon called judicial review.

Duane faced pressing problems in this first year of his five years as mayor that intertwined with the reception of *Rutgers*. Throughout the nation Patriots of property and standing were exerting themselves to recover the value of damaged or occupied real estate; rebuild destroyed houses, barns, and businesses; and receive repayment for slaves who were carried off by the British. Duane's opinion in *Rutgers* could have stalled that effort. On top of which, Duane led a city that had suffered especially demoralizing physical damage during the war years. Its lifeblood was trade, but old trade routes were closed to its overseas merchants. The streets teemed with returning Patriots, lingering Loyalists, and all manner of refugees. Keeping order was no small task. It was in part attributable to Duane's evenhandedness that the city recovered. When he left office in 1789, New York City was the center of the new nation and the home of its new federal government. In some subtle, and other not so subtle ways, *Rutgers* aided in the city's recovery, the creation of a strong union, and the rise of the doctrine of judicial review. These were its legacies.

Despite some concessions to the new nation in the Peace Treaty of 1783, Britain denied to New York merchants access to the once lucrative West Indian trade in foodstuffs. France did not open its West Indian ports to the ships of its erstwhile ally. While Hamilton and others labored to "reopen channels of commerce and credit" with Britain, in the interstices of the old empires, in trade with far-off ports of call, and up and down the Atlantic coastline, New York merchants found profitable business. At the same time, trade to the orient provided access to the Spice Islands, India, and China, and trade in tea, pepper, cinnamon, and silk. There were opportunities to exploit the fur trade of the Far West, access to the beaver and deerskins that only two decades earlier had driven the French and English to fight a seven-year war in North America. Not least, there was the City infrastructure to rebuild, churches and manufacturing establishments to refurbish, and the port itself to restore. The real estate market was booming, even though the state and City government, for the time being, was dominated by a majority unfriendly to the business community. If all else failed, there were always western lands to develop. Sears, Lamb, and their coterie's rise to power in the state did not stop the mercantile elite from resuming their speculative ways.

Called the "new New Yorkers" by modern chroniclers of these postwar boom years, newer City residents like Hamilton, Burr, and Varick were joined by English immigrants like William Duer, and Long Islanders like Melancton Smith, as well as "a procession of merchants from New England." That region, so long dependent on the sale of its fish and timber to the British Sugar Islands, had now begun its long economic decline. New York City was the new "city on a hill" for these men. So, too, Congress repaired to the city in 1785, stuffing its members into the meeting chamber in City Hall where, a year earlier, Hamilton had argued *Rutgers*. The delegates were met with "elegant festivities," and why not, since they had brought full pockets to the city's taverns and boarding houses. With peace opening the gates to the City, merchants from the West Indies, workers from Ireland, and religious sectaries from Germany also arrived. One was Archibald Gracie, a Scot in the liquor trade, then insurance, then banking. In 1891, his mansion would become the home and office of the City's mayors. Another of these immigrants was young John Jacob Astor, who would begin his family's rise to wealth by selling musical instruments and end by dominating the fur trade. Some of the newcomers brought capital. Others brought their entrepreneurial vision. Most brought a willingness to work. More people meant more need for housing, more housing meant more jobs for the draymen and carters, masons and carpenters. Merchant Elkanah Watson thought the "rebound" of the City's commerce "truly wonderful." In fact, no American city grew faster or fatter in these years than New York City.

The best of the new homes had to have elegant furniture, tableware, and tea and coffee servers. Importers saw a rising tide of business in these consumer durables. A buying spree among Americans denied access to European items during the war led to widespread personal indebtedness. This, added to the still unpaid debts of the Congress and some of the states, made finances the number one priority of the Confederation. Hamilton was especially aware of the problem, for his own financial troubles mirrored that of the nation, which did not stop him from seeking financial support from his father-in-law Philip Schuyler.

For his trouble in *Rutgers*, Hamilton earned a little over £9, but his office was busy with other clients seeking to defend themselves against the Trespass Act. Hamilton boasted to former New Yorker Gouverneur Morris that the radicals' legislative campaign was sowing so much litigation that the lawyers could hardly take time away from their practices. According to a compilation of cases in the *Law Practice of Alexander Hamilton*, he "participated" in forty-four cases involving the Trespass Act until 1791. In court, his almost hypnotic stare and "antics" of barely controlled frenzy in front of a jury engendered a kind of adoration among younger lawyers. His sociability outside of the courtroom brought him the respect of his elders. With equals he was reserved but generous. For example, Burr and Hamilton developed a friendly rivalry in court, sometimes joining forces to represent a client, more often on opposite sides. Hamilton may have been unmatched "on paper," but Burr was quicker and surer in getting to the point. Outside of court, they traded visits to one another's homes and joined in efforts to improve life in the City. Both men opposed slavery and were charter members of the New York Manumission Society, along with John Jay and other lawyers (though both men owned slaves).

Burr had married in these years, choosing an older woman whose family was hardly as prominent as Hamilton's betrothed. In consequence, Burr's finances were in greater disarray than Hamilton's. Thus Burr's law practice was even more important as a source of steady income. Part of it consisted of recovering his in-laws' loans. Chasing deadbeat debtors was not going to make Burr wealthy, however. An ever-expanding caseload, constant travel, and a budding political career left Burr slightly behind the curve that men like Hamilton were tracing. The allure of land speculation was irresistible, but land development projects, even if successful, would take years to return a profit. Burr, like Hamilton, was always in debt. But New York City after *Rutgers* was the mecca for men on the make like Hamilton and Burr.

———

As the City recovered from its wartime troubles, *Rutgers* was making its way into the thinking of the nation's lawyers. Every landmark case has an external and internal history. *Rutgers*'s external history was political in the largest sense, a part of the story of the national union. Hamilton used the case to bring together a series of ideas about the new nation and its laws, how states could cooperate, and how a central government must run. For the case was not just about real estate use, it was about who could grow the economy and who could add to the nation's store of economic stability. All of these were bound together by the larger issue of how the nation could survive its teething years.

As he tried to fit all of these ideas together, Hamilton drew on his experience before the war. Unlike the adult Burr, who was always a New Yorker first and a nationalist second, Hamilton had traveled farther and saw more. He knew firsthand how the commerce of the empire moved from port to port. In the economically troubled times of growing debt and floundering currency after the Revolutionary War, he concluded that the fate of the new republic rested on sound finances at home and investment from abroad. Never a deeply religious man and certainly not a conventional religious thinker, commerce was to him a kind of faith.

In 1784, the immediate goal was to insure that the former Loyalists and British subjects could remain in the state and litigate with some chance of winning. Over the course of arguing these cases, Hamilton's defense of these clients increasingly rested on contributions that the former Loyalists and sojourning Britons could make to the new nation. Along the way, he established a version of the committees of correspondence of 1772. Writing to and receiving letters from former revolutionary officers and members of the Congress as part of the founding of the Society of the Cincinnati, Hamilton promoted the ideals of effective national government. He also kept touch with trends in litigation, watching with special concern as local juries declined to award British merchants, their agents, or their assignees the full value of prewar debts, despite treaty provisions asking the United States to abet the collection of these outstanding debts.

As memories of the war receded, the laws of war were supplanted in Hamilton's thinking by concern for the economics and politics of the state and the nation. He hoped that therein lay an answer to both the legal questions he raised in *Rutgers* and the larger questions that *Rutgers* raised. While the City gradually improved its fortunes and the state bickered with its neighbors, elections brought moderate conservatives like Hamilton into office. In the state legislature, he promoted banking, land speculation, and tax reforms—reforms that would increase the state's revenue and provide opportunities for domestic and foreign investment. He had argued for these reforms for five years and now found himself in a position to propose them to his fellow assemblymen. He was partially successful in rectifying what he had bewailed to Gouverneur Morris as previous sessions' contrivances to "mortify and punish" former Loyalists. Against his own interest, he had a hand in repealing the portions of the 1779 law that barred Loyalist lawyers from practice. He worked assiduously to convince the manor lords and the merchant leaders that their interests were the same as the former Tories—to protect property. It was not old vested interests that Hamilton sought to promote, however; it was forward-looking capital enterprise of the sort that had made the British Empire the greatest in the world.

In the years between 1784 and 1787, Hamilton also thought long and hard about American constitutional reform. He concluded that the weakness of the financial foundations of commerce lay in the weakness of the confederation. Hamilton was well aware of the miniature tax and customs wars that states waged against one another. New York was one of the foremost offenders in this regard. These, like the Patriot-Loyalist legal combat, had carried over from the war years. In fact even in the common effort of waging war against the British, New Yorkers, New Englanders, and southerners did not see eye-to-eye on a wide variety of issues. Slavery was one of them, as were land policy, tax law, and apportionment of state legislatures. In the new states, western farmers battled with coastal merchants, debtors with creditors, and populists with conservatives over control of the state governments. New York's factious politics were hardly the most vituperative example of these combats.

In the end, Hamilton argued that the only sure way to create financial stability was to reform the Confederation. He had proposed this as early as his 1780 letter to Duane. In 1782 and again the next year he drafted proposals to place the Confederation government—hence the nation's—finances on a sounder footing. A stronger central government would attract investment from abroad and reduce the costs of interstate strife. In 1785, a conflict between Maryland and Virginia over traffic on the Potomac River served as the occasion for Virginia to call for a conference of the states to discuss similar problems. Virginia's call for a meeting at Annapolis of delegates from all the states in September 1786 brought a response from only nine of them, and only five managed to send delegates—Virginia, Delaware, New Jersey, Pennsylvania, and New York. Maryland, whose capital was the site of the conference, sent no delegates.

Hamilton attended and there greeted a former colleague from Congress, James Madison of Virginia. Their conversations strengthened a collaboration that would bear fruit in Philadelphia the next year. One might guess that they conspired to replace the Articles with a more national form of government. Whether they contemplated this goal or not, the Annapolis "Commissioners to Remedy Defects of the Federal Government" met for four days, from September 11 to 14, and Hamilton and Madison drafted the report to Congress:

"Deeply impressed . . . with the magnitude and importance of the object confided to them on this occasion, your Commissioners cannot forbear to indulge an expression of their earnest and unanimous wish, that speedy measures may be taken, to effect a general meeting, of the States, in a future Convention, for the same, and such other purposes, as the situation of public affairs, may be found to require." Something must be done, that much was clear to the self-styled commissioners. They could not or would not offer specifics but could agree, "That there are important defects in the system of the Federal Government is acknowledged by the Acts of all those States, which have concurred in the present Meeting . . . from the embarrassments which characterize the present State of our national affairs, foreign and domestic." The Revolutionaries were accustomed to holding conferences and meeting in conclaves, where "as may reasonably be supposed to merit a deliberate and candid discussion, in some mode, which will unite the Sentiments and Council's of all the States." The commissioners suggested "that a Convention of Deputies from the different States, for the special and sole purpose of entering into this investigation, and digesting a plan for supplying such defects" was appropriate. Then, proposals might be "particularized." Hamilton and Madison and the other delegates returned home, hopeful that the Congress would call for another, more fully representative, meeting.

Rutgers was running in the back of Hamilton's mind throughout the Annapolis conference. What New York's treatment of former Loyalists and British sojourners had demonstrated was the very "defect" that Hamilton and Madison cited in both "foreign and domestic affairs." There was no place for disfavored inhabitants to get a fair hearing when the state where they did business or established a residence passed unfair laws.

After the conference the Annapolis delegates were greeted with news they had long feared. In Maryland and Massachusetts long-simmering class animosity broke out in open civil disobedience. The most terrifying of these rebellions was Shays' Rebellion in Massachusetts. In it, farmers who could not pay private debts and/or their back taxes and faced foreclosure on their mortgaged lands engaged in public protests eerily similar to those of 1774. Then, angry Patriots had closed the local courts and refused to obey royal governors. Might the same farmers similarly resist the elected officials of their own state governments? "Debt relief" governments elected in seven states after 1783 tried to help the farmers by delaying the collection of taxes but nothing prevented private creditors from foreclosing on mortgages. The financial crisis grew worse when bad weather in 1784 caused widespread crop failures. By 1786, with western Massachusetts farmers losing their homesteads and the state government, dominated by eastern creditors, refusing to provide further relief, a former Continental Army captain named Daniel Shays and his allies led a tax revolt. Shays' Rebellion, as it was called, was ultimately quashed by military action in 1787, but the specter of rural unrest and local uprisings sent shivers of fear throughout the country. Warnings circulated that debt-ridden farmers in New Jersey and Virginia seemed likely to follow in the footsteps of the Massachusetts farmers, though protests stopped short of organized resistance to state government.

In the maelstrom of civil unrest, no one cited *Rutgers* as a platform for reform of government, but no one, certainly not Hamilton, had forgotten the argument for the defense. In the spring of 1787, Hamilton introduced a bill in the New York State Assembly to send delegates to the convention to revise the Articles of Confederation. He was named one of the delegates. But a month before he left for Philadelphia to take part in the constitutional convention, he proposed a bill to repeal all legislation contrary to the terms of the Peace Treaty of 1783 to the state legislature. The bill was modeled along lines that the Congress had drafted. In his address to the legislature, he tied national unity to judicial review. His motion made the treaty into a kind of multinational constitution in which former enemies— Patriot and Loyalist, American and Briton—could work together under law. His "Remarks on an Act Repealing Laws Inconsistent with the Treaty of Peace" was part of a passionate appeal for a true end to the war. "He urged the committee to consent to the passing of the bill, from the consideration, that the state of New-York was the only state to gain any thing by a strict adherence to the treaty. There was no other state in the union that had so much to expect from it." Trade, the protection of the Great Lakes frontier (along which British forces still occupied posts), and full reconciliation with former

Loyalists would follow. Hamilton disclaimed any intention to return property confiscated during the war, and (somewhat disingenuously) insisted that there was no law still on the books that would be struck off (though the Trespass Act was still there).

The Articles of Confederation Congress had proposed the step, even drafting model legislation for the states. Hamilton proposed that New York should lead the way adopting it, for if "this state should not come into the measure, would it not be a very good plea for the other states to favor their own citizens, and say why should we do this?" In other words, if New York passed the law, it would bring the states together, promote uniformity, and end confusion. In what amounted to little more than an aside, he brought *Rutgers* into the argument. "He declared that the full operation of the bill, would be no more than merely to declare the treaty the law of the land. And that the judges viewing it as such, shall do away all laws that may appear in direct contravention of it."

————

Hamilton and his family arrived early in Philadelphia, on May 18. He was a member of the committee selected by George Washington, the presiding officer at the convention, to draw up rules of proceeding, but otherwise his presence in the early days left little mark on the convention debates. The other delegates from New York, John Lansing and Abraham Yates, were Governor Clinton's allies. Hamilton was outvoted whenever the issue of the creation of a stronger central government arose. Perhaps in part because of this, when Hamilton gave his only major speech in Philadelphia on June 18, he vented his frustration with the course of the debates. A close reading of it shows the way in which his briefs for *Rutgers* had shaped his thinking.

Hamilton's reputation in the courtroom had preceded him as he rose to speak. The delegates could expect an oration ornamented with learning, delivered with passion, and uncompromisingly argued. He did not disappoint. He spoke for five hours without a break, for anyone else a marathon, for him little more than a training run. Years later, some of those who heard him that day and others who recalled firsthand accounts were less than admiring about the content of the oration. The final hour of the oration proposed an elected monarchy.

Had Hamilton stopped at the end of his analysis of the weakness of the plans that other delegates proposed, his speech's reputation would have been different. But he found that the so-called New Jersey Plan retained too many of the features of the confederation, and the so-called Virginia Plan did not confer on the new government the energy and discretion it would need.

Setting aside the last hour, his detailed and accurate assessment of the weakness of the confederation brought together all of the concerns he first raised in *Rutgers*. For Hamilton's real concern was the same that he faced in *Rutgers*—factions in the states, and the ill effect that these factions had upon economic growth and political harmony in the nation. Hamilton knew that political animosities had fueled the New York State legislation against the Loyalists after peace had been achieved. Such factiousness had nearly destroyed liberty in the state. Though his comments were obliquely directed at them, his fellow New York delegates sat quietly as he spoke. They would depart Philadelphia on July 10 and not return. Determined to oppose the Constitution, they wrote to Clinton that they could not support a plan that would not "afford that security to equal and permanent liberty which we wished to make an invariable object of our pursuit."

Yates in particular was struck by Hamilton's long oration, giving it more detail in his notes on the debates than any of the other speeches. According to Yates's notes, Hamilton began, "My situation is disagreeable, but it would be criminal not to come forward on a question of such magnitude. I have well considered the subject, and am convinced that no amendment of the confederation can answer the purpose of a good government, so long as State sovereignties do, in any shape, exist." Madison's notes on the speech were equally detailed. According to Madison, who was far more sympathetic to Hamilton than Yates, Hamilton said that he "had been hitherto silent on the business before the Convention, partly from respect to others whose superior abilities age & experience rendered him unwilling to bring forward ideas dissimilar to theirs, and partly from his delicate situation with respect to his own State, to whose sentiments as expressed by his Colleagues, he could by no means accede." He now decided to break his silence because "the crisis however which now marked our affairs, was too serious to permit any scruples whatever to prevail over the duty imposed on every man to contribute his efforts for the public safety & happiness."

According to Madison, Hamilton "was . . . fully convinced, that no amendment of the Confederation, leaving the States in possession of their Sovereignty could possibly answer the purpose." The uncurbed and partisan sovereignty expressed in the New York Trespass Act violated the treaty of peace. Hamilton assumed that everyone at the convention should have known that the weakness of the confederation government suborned all manner of corruption and disorder, the greatest promoter of which was the uncontrollable appetite of radical state legislation. Left to itself it would swallow all individual rights. Why could the delegates not see this?

Behind defenders of state sovereignty's "distinctions & reasonings too subtle" lay local interest, self-interest, state interests—too much liberty amounting to a species of political licentiousness. Hamilton could not deny the fact that "The States sent us here to provide for the exigencies of the Union," but he turned the limitations of the charge the state legislatures had given the delegates into a command for thorough reform. New York had not even conceded that much of its sovereignty when it instructed its delegates to the convention. They were merely told to examine various plans to remedy the Articles.

Hamilton set aside the state legislature's instructions in favor of the far stronger Annapolis Conference report. He told the delegates that "to rely on & propose any plan not adequate to these exigencies, merely because it was not clearly within our powers [that is, the state's instructions to its delegates], would be to sacrifice the means to the end." Forget about the instructions the Congress had issued. They were faulty. "It may be said that the States can not ratify a plan not within the purview of the article of Confederation providing for alterations & amendments." But no matter, for here the delegates might take the liberty of proposing an entirely new structure of government, "in view [of] a reference to the people at large." Pounding away at his central thesis, Hamilton continued that a confederation in which state sovereignty went uncompromised and uncontrolled was doomed, for the states "constantly pursue internal interests adverse to those of the whole." He did not mention the Loyalist Code in New York, but Lansing and Yates knew exactly what Hamilton meant when it said that such "internal interests" were perfect examples of "all the passions then we see, of avarice, ambition, interest, which govern most individuals, and all public bodies, fall into the current of the States."

Hamilton's solution was simple: dump state sovereignty. Only in a general government would Americans find safety from these narrow-minded partisanships. Madison reported that Hamilton "was persuaded that great oeconomy might be obtained by substituting a general Govt. He did not mean however to shock the public opinion by proposing such a measure. On the other hand he saw no other necessity for declining it." The states were not "necessary for any of the great purposes of commerce, revenue, or agriculture." A division of the whole into "Subordinate authorities he was aware would be necessary but . . . the vast & expensive apparatus now appertaining to the States" was a luxury that a nation faced with internal disorder and external enemies could not afford.

Hamilton went further, and in so doing applied the lessons he thought *Rutgers* taught. Indeed, the most rational way to explain the next part of his speech is by putting it in the context of *Rutgers*. "In his private opinion he had no scruple in declaring, supported as he was by the opinions of so many of the wise & good, that the British Govt. was the best in the world: and that he doubted much whether anything short of it would do in America." In front of an audience of former revolutionary politicians, this was an almost unbelievable admission. It had little hope of persuading anyone. Though "he hoped Gentlemen of different opinions would bear with him in this, and begged them to recollect the change of opinion on this subject which had taken place and was still going on," perhaps a reference to the more conservative second round of state constitution writing then taking place, the silence that had fallen over the chamber must have been deafening.

Over the long course of the oration Hamilton had metamorphosed from a politician at a convention to a lawyer in a courtroom. His closing words should be read as if he were in summation of a losing case before a hostile jury. So he threw it all in: "To the proper adjustment of it the British owe the excellence of their Constitution."

Once praised by Enlightenment political theorists like Montesquieu and Voltaire and extolled by Loyalists who gloried in the successes of British arms and the excellence of British laws, the very mention of Britain was now distasteful to the company surrounding Hamilton. Madison must have been squirming, his own opinions of national government not far from Hamilton's, but their common aim endangered by Hamilton's reference to the former imperial master. Hamilton now went about as far as he could safely go into the English example, or perhaps too far. For he left the valuable lessons of *Rutgers* behind in calling for an elective monarchy. It was a bridge too far—from defending Loyalist interests in postwar New York to defending an elective monarchy in Philadelphia just three years later. That suggestion undermined his "sketch of a plan" including a consolidated national government in which the states would be administrative districts. "He was aware that it went beyond the ideas of most members." That was an understatement. But the alternative he foresaw was a "Union dissolving or already dissolved." Hamilton finished with the fading light, and if he registered the response of the delegates (for he did not always allow himself to take others' feelings into account), he might have seen the dismay on their faces. A faint scattering of applause closed the session.

In his notes for the next day's debate, Yates recorded that Hamilton modified his stance: "I did not intend yesterday a total extinguishment of State governments; but my meaning was, that a national government ought to be able to support itself without the aid or interference of the State governments, and that therefore it was necessary to have full sovereignty. Even with corporate rights the States will be dangerous to the national government, and ought to be extinguished, new modified, or reduced to a smaller scale." Perhaps his passion had cooled; certainly the reception given his speech gave Hamilton pause. But though his proposals for a lifetime executive and his desire to abolish state governments seemed to be what delegates remembered of his speech, these were not real concerns. No one was going to subscribe to a constitution that created an elective kingship or did away with the states' sovereignty. He had lost cases in court before this, and losing did not mean the end of the world. On June 30, he returned to New York, and except for a brief visit on August

13, did not rejoin the delegates until September 6. Two days later he served with his fellow nationalists Gouverneur Morris, Rufus King, and Madison on the Committee of Style and Arrangement. (The fifth member, William Samuel Johnson of Connecticut, was a lawyer much in the Egbert Benson mold.) No doubt with Hamilton's help, Morris refashioned the draft into the seven Articles and rewrote the Preamble. Subtly, perhaps even slyly, the committee turned a constitution that began "We the people of the states of [there followed a list of the states] . . . do ordain, declare, and establish the following constitution" into one whose preamble read "We the People of the United States, in order to form a more perfect union." If the Constitution still made concessions to state sovereignty, the Preamble augured the sort of Union that Hamilton wanted.

Rutgers played into Hamilton's notion of federalism during the ratification debates. Hamilton connected the lack of respect (always a personal as well as a political matter for him) accorded the new nation by its European peers with the endemic weakness of the confederation. The Federalist Papers were a series of newspaper articles that Hamilton, Madison, and Jay wrote to aid the ratification of the constitution in New York. In Federalist Number 15, published December 1, 1787, Hamilton railed against the "national humiliation" that failure to obey international law had brought down on the confederation. "Are we even in a condition to remonstrate with dignity? The just imputations on our own faith, in respect to the same treaty, ought first to be removed." He was still arguing *Rutgers* three years after the decision came down, against Americans who behaved like the depraved monarchs of old, when "little dependence [could be] placed on treaties which have no other sanction than the obligations of good faith, and which oppose general considerations of peace and justice to the impulse of any immediate interest or passion." Such narrow-minded partisanship had fueled the passage of the Trespass Act, with its attendant violation of the Treaty of Peace.

In Federalist Number 33, appearing on January 2, 1788, Hamilton discoursed particularly on the Supremacy Clause of Article VI, providing "that the Constitution and the laws of the United States made in pursuance thereof, and the treaties made by their authority shall be the supreme law of the land, any thing in the constitution or laws of any State to the contrary notwithstanding." The language tracked closely the claims and the rhetoric he used in *Rutgers*. At that time, the treaty-making body was the confederation's Congress, a point he raised in the Federalist piece. He noted with some asperity the "virulent" and "petulant" invective directed by antifederalists at that clause, castigating it "as the pernicious engine by which their local governments were to be destroyed and their liberties exterminated." This was exactly what the defenders of the Trespass Act had argued when *Rutgers* was decided.

In what should be regarded as a reference to the work of the Committee of Style and Arrangement on which Hamilton sat, and which composed the final version of the Constitution, Hamilton continued that "the Convention probably foresaw, what it has been a principal aim of these papers to inculcate, that the danger which most threatens our political welfare is that the State governments will finally sap the foundations of the Union." With this sweeping (if not entirely accurate) depiction of the convention members' thinking, Hamilton made them into co-authors of *Phocion* and co-counsel for the defense in *Rutgers*.

In Federalist Number 80, published on June 21, 1788, Hamilton returned to the question of treaty obligations, the debt, and the necessity of a federal judicial system. Again *Rutgers* was lurking in the shadows of his argument.

> The Union will undoubtedly be answerable to foreign powers for the conduct of its members. And the responsibility for an injury ought ever to be accompanied with the faculty of preventing it. As the denial or perversion of justice by the sentences of courts, as well as in any other manner, is with reason classed among the just causes of war, it will follow that the federal judiciary ought to have cognizance of all causes in which the citizens of other countries are concerned.

By "any other manner" Hamilton meant legislative infringements of justice like the Trespass Act.

Hamilton's doppelganger in all of this was silent throughout the convention deliberations. Aaron Burr could have been a delegate had he wished. Judge Yates had been chosen, attended, and then left, seeing the direction of the deliberations and rejecting it. Had Burr been chosen, would he have engaged in such a dramatic gesture? It was not like him. He would have stayed the course. Though he was not a deep political thinker like Hamilton, he grasped the nub of questions in the courtroom and would have in the Philadelphia convention debates. Did Burr see the hand of the manager of Waddington's defense in the emerging document? Of course he did. Burr's name was proposed for the New York State ratification convention, but he took out a newspaper advertisement declining any nomination, thus avoiding any direct confrontation with Hamilton at the ratification convention. Such a confrontation would have been unavoidable, for Hamilton spoke often and long in Poughkeepsie. Burr consented to serve as one of New York's senators in the new Congress, and unlike his virtually invisible service in the state legislature, in the Senate Burr was a valuable and visible lieutenant in the emerging Democratic Republican Party. The Republicans opposed Hamilton's domestic policy initiatives. The party wars of New York thus came to the U.S. Congress. Over the course of the next decade, Hamilton would allow his simmering rivalry with Burr to explode into episodes of public denunciation as the two men reenacted *Rutgers'* arguments about the sovereignty of states and the supremacy of central government on the new stage of national politics.

Despite the inauguration of the federalist government that Hamilton supported so ardently in the ratification debates, *Rutgers*-like problems remained sticking points in the repayment of debts owed the British under the treaty. With state courts still favoring debtors, British merchants turned to the federal Congress to keep the promises that the confederation Congress had made. With the states' courts and state sovereignty reluctant to obey the treaty provisions, as New York State had been in passing the Trespass Act, the British relied on the Treaty Clause of the federal Constitution. On January 19, 1791, discussing the treaty relations with France, Secretary of State Thomas Jefferson told the U.S. Senate, "stipulations by treaty are forever irrevocable but by joint consent, let a change of circumstances render them ever so burdensome." While the immediate question might have been commercial relations with France, Jefferson had not forgotten the terms of the Peace Treaty of 1783. He did not want the debt to become a perpetual burden on the American people, but he also favored a limited version of federalism. Hamilton, by contrast, wanted to pay off the private debts along with the public debt.

On April 26, 1792, George Hammond, the British ambassador to the United States, wrote to Jefferson, citing case law favoring honoring of the spirit as well as the letter of the treaty: "All the cases, to which you have alluded (excepting that of *Rutgers v. Waddington*, which was printed at New York) have been collected from the manuscript notes of a *friend*, and I have no doubt of their being accurately reported." Jefferson's evasive, self-serving, and mischievous answer came on May 29, 1792. In a series of bulleted items, Jefferson dismissed or diminished Hammond's concern: "that Compensation by the British treasury, to British sufferers, was the alternative of her own choice, our negotiators having offered to do that if she would compensate such losses as we had sustained by acts authorized by the modern & moderate principles of war"; that in America state "Judges & Jurors, are to decide in their discretion, & are accordingly in the habit of augmenting, diminishing or refusing interest in every case, according to their discretion"; that nothing in the treaty provided for interest on the unpaid debts; that the courts were always open to the British claimants, and "that the decisions of courts & juries against the claims of interest, are too probably founded, to give cause for questioning their integrity." Jefferson virtually ignored the way in which state laws had denied to the British full recompense, and state courts had chancered (set off against credits) the amounts of the debt or permitted it be paid in paper currency or nearly valueless lands. Jefferson then spent the next year hounding Hammond about the British occupation of the Great Lakes forts.

Hammond was not amused, indeed felt "put upon" by Jefferson's attitude, and reported back to Lord Grenville on June 8, 1792,

> The great quantity of irrelevant matter contained in [the letter from Jefferson], the positive denial of many facts, which I had advanced upon the authority of the British agents and of other respectable persons in this country, the unjustifiable insinuations thrown out with respect to the mode of prosecuting the war, and

to the conduct of his Majesty's ministers subsequent to the peace, and the general acrimonious stile and manner of this letter, all contributed to excite in me considerable surprize.

Correspondence between the two men never settled the issues that Hamilton had raised in his briefs for *Rutgers*.

What is more, Hammond's "friend," it turned out, was none other than Secretary of the Treasury Hamilton. Setting aside the question of whether Hamilton acted unethically or even illegally in passing information on cabinet meetings to Hammond, Hamilton had already weighed in on the question of state sovereignty and federal treaty-making powers. Though his views had not changed since 1784 or 1788, as secretary of the treasury in Washington's first administration Hamilton was busy trying to interest British investors in American business, and this altered the context of his relationship with the British interest. Hammond was his conduit to the potential investors. He hoped that foreign investment would not only promote American manufactures, but pull together even more securely an Atlantic-world network of people of means. Only when capital underwrote the federal government could it achieve the financial dominance over the states that he had proposed nearly a decade earlier. The ratification of the Constitution was a step in this direction, and his program of funding and assumption of the outstanding state war debts, the creation of a national bank, and federal support for new industries was a further step.

With the project of engaging British investors in the finances of the new nation, Hamilton once more turned to his core arguments in *Rutgers*. Aware that Hammond was soon to broach the question of unpaid debts with Jefferson, Hamilton wrote to Jefferson on April 16, 1792:

> The fact was that the defendant had occupied the brewhouse in question, under regular authority of the British army, proceeding for a part of the time, immediately from the commander in chief, and for another part of it, from the Qr. Master General, and had even paid rent for the use of it. . . . The force of the treaty to overrule the inhibition against pleading a military order, was admitted

by the decision, which allowed in fact the validity of such an order, when proceeding from the commander in chief.

Hamilton added that he had acted as "attorney and counsel for the defendant" and that Hammond had correctly presented the facts in correspondence with Jefferson. *Rutgers* remained at the center of this controversy nearly ten years after the Peace Treaty of 1783 was ratified.

Hamilton's view would win a temporary vindication in *Ware v. Hylton* (1796), in which the Supreme Court held that British creditors could not be barred from bringing suits for prewar debts by state laws, and finally won the day in *State of Missouri v. Holland* (1920). In it, Justice Oliver Wendell Holmes Jr. found that a treaty between Great Britain and the United States, and pursuant to it, congressional regulation of the hunting of migratory birds, trumped a Missouri law. "Treaties made under the authority of the United States, along with the Constitution and laws of the United States made in pursuance thereof, are declared the supreme law of the land. If the treaty is valid, there can be no dispute about the validity of the statute under Article I, § 8, as a necessary and proper means to execute the powers of the Government."

———

The internal history of *Rutgers* takes us in a different direction—to its legacy as an example of "judicial review." Judicial review is a judge-made claim that courts can find legislation unconstitutional and therefore void. The court lays the text of the statute against the text of the constitution and finds a contradiction. That part of the statute then falls. Judicial review stands on the independence of courts from the other branches, hence it is most likely to appear in cases where a statute limits what the court may do. That was true in *Rutgers*, where the Trespass Act forbade defendants to offer military necessity as a defense to the claim for damages. Duane did not limit his discussion of the court review of the constitutionality of the statute to its impact on the courts, however.

In American constitutional law, the doctrine is usually associated with Chief Justice John Marshall's opinion for the U.S. Supreme

Court in *Marbury v. Madison* (1803). It, too, concerned a case in which a statute, the Judiciary Act of 1789, added to the Court's original jurisdiction a power not in Article III's description of the Court's original jurisdiction. In a unanimous opinion, the Court found that part of the statute violated the federal Constitution. Marshall wrote

> It is emphatically the province and duty of the Judicial Department [the judicial branch] to say what the law is. . . . So, if a law [e.g., a statute or treaty] be in opposition to the Constitution, if both the law and the Constitution apply to a particular case, so that the Court must either decide that case conformably to the law, disregarding the Constitution, or conformably to the Constitution, disregarding the law, the Court must determine which of these conflicting rules governs the case. This is of the very essence of judicial duty. If, then, the Courts are to regard the Constitution, and the Constitution is superior to any ordinary act of the Legislature, the Constitution, and not such ordinary act, must govern the case to which they both apply.

Scholars and jurists have debated where Marshall found the authority for this pronouncement. One answer may be section 25 of the Judiciary Act of 1789. This gave the Supreme Court the authority to review state court decisions and legislation affecting the Constitution when such decisions were appealed. But where did this portion of the enabling act come from? One answer is that, like much in the Constitution, precedent for judicial review came from the judicial experience of the states. After *Rutgers* was decided and Duane's opinion was published in pamphlet form—in fact because Duane's opinion was published in full—a number of other state courts raised the issue of judicial review explicitly. The occasion, as in *Rutgers*, was a statute that limited what courts could do or prescribed forms of procedure that appeared to be at variance with the state constitution.

The first of these was *Symsbury's Case* (1785) in Connecticut. Connecticut had not prepared a state constitution during the revolution. It retained its colonial charter. These charters were not fundamental law in the revolutionary sense because they were not crafted by a convention chosen by the people nor ratified by the people. They were frames of government granted to the colony as privileges by the crown. The Connecticut charter was nonetheless regarded as a constitution by the state government.

The case itself revolved around a survey of the boundaries of adjacent towns. Such disputed boundaries, often involving valuable stands of timber or access to river courses, constantly vexed relations among New England townspeople. Here, a 1727 survey was accepted by the legislature and imposed on a landholder whose title predated the survey. The court preferred a common law rule basing ownership on the date of the grant of land. The charter provided that the people "shall have and enjoy all Liberties and Immunities of free born natural Subjects within any the Dominions of US, Our Heirs or Successors, to all Intents, Constructions and Purposes whatsoever, as if they and every of them were born within the realm of England." That included the common law. The assembly could "from Time to Time to Make, Ordain, and Establish all manner of wholesome, and reasonable Laws Statutes, Ordinances, Directions, and Instructions, not Contrary to the Laws of this Realm of England." In effect, the court determined, in the course of finding for the earlier claim under the charter, that the legislative act was inoperative. Resolving boundary disputes was the job of the courts, not the legislature. Although the outcome of the case depended on this ruling, the ruling did not state nor did it rest on a wholesale doctrine of judicial review.

Next in time were the New Hampshire *Ten-Pound Act Cases*. The state constitution provided for a right to jury trial in "all" cases "concerning property." In 1785, the legislature's Ten-Pound Act allowed justices of peace sitting without juries to hear and decide certain kinds of actions involving debt and trespass without a jury if the amount in question was less than ten pounds state money. Again, in unrecorded opinions in 1786 and 1787, county courts found that the statute did not comport with the constitution, and the statute was repealed. Newspaper accounts of the cases are the only evidence of the cases, however, so the logic of the court was not recorded. All of the three elements of Duane's opinion—that the Constitution controlled the legislature, that the courts could interpret the meaning of the constitution, and that the act violated the constitution—seem to have been present.

Trevett v. Weeden (1786) in Rhode Island raised issues similar to

Rutgers, though again the state had maintained its old charter rather than writing a new constitution, and the brief that James Varnum, defendant's counsel, wrote that a statute dispensing with juries violated basic common law precepts guaranteed by the Rhode Island constitution. Varnum published his brief as a pamphlet, and it circulated widely. His argument persuaded two of the three judges on the panel. The legislature demanded an explanation from the judges. The case had thus become a clear test of separation of powers in which judicial review was a part. Summoned, the judges refused to explain themselves, and the crisis passed without resolution.

Symsbury, the *Ten-Pound Act Cases*, and *Trevett* can be read as endorsements of judicial review. In all three cases, however, the court refused to entertain the general question of whether courts could lay a piece of legislation against the constitution and find the former void. It was not that the judges skirted this view. They simply refused to engage in constitutional or doctrinal analysis. They did not see it as their task to do so. They were simply tasked with adjudicating disputes.

The last of this sequence of cases was *Bayard v. Singleton* (1787), a North Carolina suit in which plaintiff's claim to a piece of land rested upon a former Loyalist's title. In it, James Iredell, counsel for the defendant, explored judicial review frankly. Iredell was a future U.S. Supreme Court justice, and because of that, his published comments have gained greater significance than they might otherwise have had.

Confederation-era politics in North Carolina were toxic and one source of the poison was the cantankerous chief justice of the supreme court, Samuel Ashe. Some of the vituperation that surfaced in his jurisprudence was personal, stemming from patronage and other like causes, but state politics were also riven by real differences of opinion about the future of the nation. Ashe was hard on the former Loyalists, in the process antagonizing conservative leaders of the bar like James Iredell, Archibald Maclaine, and William Hooper. Like Hamilton in New York, the latter two had built up practices defending the former Loyalists. In 1785, however, the legislature passed a judiciary act forbidding the lower courts from hearing former Loyalist claims for property confiscated under an earlier law. Although the court in *Bayard* found that the legislation was defective, it instructed the jury that the original Loyalist owner had forfeited the right to the land, after which the jury brought in a verdict for the defendant because the former Loyalist no longer had title.

It was in this context that Iredell wrote a "Letter to the Public" in the Newbern newspaper under the pseudonym "Elector." His tone was admonitory. "The abuse of unlimited power" in the legislature was controlled with great wisdom in the state's constitution. It did not limit redress for abuse of power to future elections or the forbearance of the assembly itself, to petition, or to insurrection. Instead, the appropriate means to curb an unconstitutional act was for the judiciary to determine the application of the law. "An act of the assembly inconsistent with the constitution is void" and it was the "duty" of the courts to say so. The legislature could not say to the county courts that they lacked the jurisdiction to hear cases that, in the public good, should be heard. Iredell did not limit his logic to those statutes that interfered with the courts, but in this case, the parallel to Duane's reasoning in *Rutgers* is too obvious to miss.

———

Although some of the state cases were well enough known at the time, they did not spur a thorough discussion of judicial supremacy at the constitutional convention. Discussion of courts and of Article III was the briefest of all three branches' roles. There were passing mentions of judicial review of statutes' constitutionality (without anyone using the term). Pennsylvania's John Dickinson, a lawyer with a huge practice, opined that judges should not have the authority to void a law. On the other side, Massachusetts delegate and future antifederalist Elbridge Gerry told the convention (according to Madison's notes) that judges must be able to "check against encroachments on their own department by their exposition of the laws, which involved a power of deciding on their constitutionality." Hamilton's long address, already discussed under the rubric of the external history of *Rutgers*, did not mention judicial review.

Hamilton got the chance to explain his view of the matter in his Federalist newspaper essays. Hamilton correctly anticipated opposition to Article III of the Constitution in the New York ratification convention, led by the very same Melancton Smith who criticized

Duane for usurping the powers of the legislature. In this instance, Hamilton's Federalist Number 22 opened the way to a defense of judicial review. It appeared in the newspapers on December 14, 1787. The essay afforded Hamilton a chance to rehearse the defects of the confederation and the dangerous state in which the new nation found itself. He sounded all the alarms: finance and commerce were imperiled by the weakness of the Congress. Foreign powers took advantage of these weaknesses to make the United States a least-favored trading partner. Last but hardly least in his thinking was the want of a central, authoritative judicial power: "A circumstance which crowns the defects of the Confederation remains yet to be mentioned, the want of a judiciary power. Laws are a dead letter without courts to expound and define their true meaning and operation." It was his immediate segue into the treaty power of the proposed federal government that showed how *Rutgers* was, to use a modern analogy, still running in Hamilton's random access memory. "The treaties of the United States, to have any force at all, must be considered as part of the law of the land. Their true import, as far as respects individuals, must, like all other laws, be ascertained by judicial determinations." Hamilton then applied the lesson to the draft Article III. "To produce uniformity in these determinations, they ought to be submitted, in the last resort, to one SUPREME TRIBUNAL. And this tribunal ought to be instituted under the same authority which forms the treaties themselves." At which point, Hamilton left a fuller discussion of the judiciary for a later time.

That time came on the eve of the New York State ratification convention. Burr, by choice, was absent. Though his name appeared on the New York County ballot, he took out an advertisement in the local papers to say that it appeared without his knowledge. By his friendships, patronage, and legal business one can surmise that he was an opponent of the new constitution, but he never gave a speech or wrote in public against it. Still, held in Poughkeepsie in the region dominated by antifederalists like Governor Clinton and Melancton Smith, it might well have gone down to defeat. Ratification in New York was vital to the new Constitution's future.

Trying to sway public opinion in New York, Hamilton assayed a new series of Federalist papers. Number 78 appeared on June 14,

1788, within weeks of the meeting of the ratification convention. Hamilton had delayed his discussion of the judiciary until the last moment. In one sense, Article III should have been the easiest of all the provisions to defend. "In unfolding the defects of the existing Confederation, the utility and necessity of a federal judicature have been clearly pointed out." Hamilton had done so in Federalist Number 22, if authority for that statement was needed. No one need fear such arrangements, for

> whoever attentively considers the different departments of power must perceive, that, in a government in which they are separated from each other, the judiciary, from the nature of its functions, will always be the least dangerous to the political rights of the Constitution; because it will be least in a capacity to annoy or injure them. The Executive not only dispenses the honors, but holds the sword of the community. The legislature not only commands the purse, but prescribes the rules by which the duties and rights of every citizen are to be regulated. The judiciary, on the contrary, has no influence over either the sword or the purse; no direction either of the strength or of the wealth of the society; and can take no active resolution whatever. It may truly be said to have neither FORCE nor WILL, but merely judgment.

But the defense of the federal judiciary was not so easy, because Hamilton wanted it to include a proposition anathema to many of the delegates who would assemble in Poughkeepsie that summer— judicial review. Hamilton's rhetorical skills were stretched to their limits to accomplish this aim.

He began with the proposition that the very weakness of the judiciary required that "all possible care is requisite to enable it to defend itself against . . . attacks [from the other branches] . . . the general liberty of the people can never be endangered from that quarter; I mean so long as the judiciary remains truly distinct from both the legislature and the Executive." Ingeniously, Hamilton had introduced the notion of judicial review by hiding it in the middle of a defense of the tenure of the judges, an entirely different subject, and girding judicial review with the armor of checks and balances. For how could the judiciary maintain its independence of judgment, so necessary to liberty, if it were told how to proceed by the other branches or its members punished by those branches for exercising independent judgment?

Then, by a sleight of hand, Hamilton brought judicial review out of hiding: "Limitations of this kind [on the other branches] can be preserved in practice no other way than through the medium of courts of justice, whose duty it must be to declare all acts contrary to the manifest tenor of the Constitution void. Without this, all the reservations of particular rights or privileges would amount to nothing." Judicial review is the logical consequence of superior, foundational principles like separation of powers, not the primary assertion in these passages. Hamilton knew firsthand that judicial review on its own was unpopular, especially in New York (the intended audience for the Federalist essays). Often impolitic in his pleading, Hamilton here was the soul of political astuteness.

Having laid the foundation for a full defense of judicial review, Hamilton pressed his case for it.

> There is no position which depends on clearer principles, than that every act of a delegated authority, contrary to the tenor of the commission under which it is exercised, is void. No legislative act, therefore, contrary to the Constitution, can be valid. To deny this, would be to affirm, that the deputy is greater than his principal; that the servant is above his master; that the representatives of the people are superior to the people themselves; that men acting by virtue of powers, may do not only what their powers do not authorize, but what they forbid.

And the courts were the institution whose independent judgment best carried out this task. Legislators may claim themselves to be the better interpreter of their own laws, and of the constitution, for they were the elected representatives of the people. But this view was fallacious.

> It is far more rational to suppose, that the courts were designed to be an intermediate body between the people and the legislature, in order, among other things, to keep the latter within the limits

assigned to their authority. The interpretation of the laws is the proper and peculiar province of the courts. A constitution is, in fact, and must be regarded by the judges, as a fundamental law. It therefore belongs to them to ascertain its meaning, as well as the meaning of any particular act proceeding from the legislative body.

Hamilton then closed the discussion of judicial review by returning to the need for life tenure. He did this in a single sentence—suggesting that a defense of the former, rather than the latter, was his purpose all along.

It is not surprising to discover that Hamilton's effort to domesticate judicial review ran into serious criticism at the New York ratification convention. After all, all of the cases in which courts invalidated the whole or a part of state legislation ran into some kind of backlash from the legislature and in the press. Even Hamilton's sometime collaborator James Madison had doubts, which he expressed privately to Thomas Jefferson. In his memo "Observations on Jefferson's Draft of a Constitution for Virginia" sent to Jefferson on October 15, 1788, when Madison had led the effort in the Virginia ratification convention to approve the Constitution, he warned that

> in the State Constitutions & indeed in the Fedl. one also, no provision is made for the case of a disagreement in expounding them; and as the Courts are generally the last in making their decision, it results to them, by refusing or not refusing to execute a law, to stamp it with its final character. This makes the Judiciary Dept paramount in fact to the Legislature, which was never intended, and can never be proper.

Never? Well, hardly ever. For one further piece of evidence suggests that despite Madison's and others' objections, the Hamiltonian idea of judicial review had found a place in the new Constitution. Article III's first clause read "the judicial Power of the United States, shall be vested in one supreme Court, and in such inferior Courts as the Congress may from time to time ordain and establish." Pursuant to this provision, Congress passed the Judiciary Act of 1789. Its section 25 provided

> that a final judgment or decree in any suit, in the highest court of law or equity of a State in which a decision in the suit could be had, where is drawn in question the validity of a treaty or statute of, or an authority exercised under the United States, and the decision is against their validity; or where is drawn in question the validity of a statute of, or an authority exercised under any State, on the ground of their being repugnant to the constitution, treaties or laws of the United States, and the decision is in favour of such their validity, or where is drawn in question the construction of any clause of the constitution, or of a treaty, or statute of, or commission held under the United States, and the decision is against the title, right, privilege or exemption specially set up or claimed by either party, under such clause of the said Constitution, treaty, statute or commission, may be re-examined and reversed or affirmed in the Supreme Court of the United States upon a writ of error.

Hamilton had no direct hand in writing this passage. It was the work of Oliver Ellsworth and the members of the Senate committee that drafted the act. But Ellsworth and Hamilton were both in New York City serving in the new federal government when the act was framed, both had served in the Constitutional Convention, and both were strong federalists. Surely the two men met often enough in the enlarged former City Hall, in 1789 transformed into Federal Hall, where both houses of Congress sat when the act was being debated. Opponents of the section recognized that it flowed from the federalists' view of judicial review at the convention and from Hamilton's defense of judicial review in the Federalist Papers. After the adoption of section 25, as historian Daniel Hulsebosch has written, "in the federal courts, judicial review of state legislation for the benefit of Britons became uncontroversial." According to Hulsebosch, whose work on incorporation of international law in the Constitution is persuasive on this point, Ellsworth wanted the U.S. Supreme Court to protect foreign litigants against the bias of state courts as well as state legislatures—extending the concept of judicial review from a separation of powers doctrine to a fact of federalism.

However deployed and defended, judicial review was never a popular doctrine. John Marshall's masterful treatment of it in *Marbury v. Madison* (1803) may have stood on the shoulders of state precedent, but after it was decided he and it were attacked on very similar grounds to the criticism of *Rutgers* nineteen years earlier. Jeffersonian Republicans orchestrated this chorus of opposition as part of their campaign to rid the public arena of Federalist influence. But another element of the opposition came from those who saw legislation as the only true expression of republican governance. In this view, courts should stick to adjudicating individual cases and not act as miniature legislatures. That same argument continues to infuse modern attacks on judicial review. Despite the criticism then and now, judicial review is a part of appellate courts' powers throughout the nation, and more telling, is now seen as a protection of individual rights. As the New York State Court of Appeals pronounced in *People v. Guthrie* (2015), the appeals courts of the state look to judicial review to further "the protection of the individual rights of our citizens."

———

For some scholars, the coming of the federal Constitution represented a conservative backlash against the radical inclinations of some of the Revolutionaries. The case can be made for Hamilton at least. As he wrote to Robert Livingston on April 25, 1785, "the situation of the state at this time is so critical that it is become a serious object of attention to those who are concerned for the *security of property* or the prosperity of government, to endeavour to put men in the Legislature whose principles are not of the *levelling kind*. The spirit of the present Legislature is truly alarming, and appears evidently directed to the confusion of all property and principle" [italics in original]. If the conventional reading of Hamilton's views supports this counterrevolution thesis, many of those revolutionary luminaries who objected to the Constitution, for example Patrick Henry in Virginia, were just as concerned that property and property rights be protected by law. They just did not trust the federal government to provide this protection.

Instead, the real issue then as today is states' rights. Hamilton feared the disunity and disorder inherent in states' sovereignty theories. The Constitution compromised on the issue of state sovereignty, as did the Bill of Rights, leaving the states' legislatures and courts in control over the great mass of credit and debt cases. It would be many years before the federal courts deployed the interstate commerce clause, the taxation clause, and then the Fourteenth Amendment to leech away the jurisdiction of the states in this area.

But the framers of the Constitution did not compromise on the importance of private property. As James Madison explained in Federalist Number 10, "the first object of government" for the federalists was "the protection of and unequal faculties of acquiring property." Madison was a rich man, coming from a wealthy family, and for him "unequal faculties" amounted to the rich protecting their property from the masses. Madison was about as far from being an advocate of a more egalitarian distribution of wealth as Gouverneur Morris, the manor lord of Morrisania on the Hudson, who had as much to do with the final shape of the Constitution as anyone in Philadelphia. Later in life, Morris expanded Madison's legal formula into a social axiom: "Property was the main object of society . . . which could only be secured by the restraints of regular government." Morris, as it happened, had also brought a suit under the Trespass Act to the Mayor's Court: *Morris v. Hallet*, filed on February 10, 1784. There Morris won £980 damages in lieu of back rent.

Epilogue

Rutgers v. Waddington and the Second American Civil War

Civil wars are bloodthirsty affairs. From the ancient Roman civil wars through the English civil wars of the 1640s historical records amply demonstrate the winners' unkindness to the losers after open hostilities ended. But the civil war at the heart of the American Revolution did not follow that pattern. Early leaders of the French Revolution like the Marquis de Lafayette fulsomely cited the influence and precedent of the American Revolution on the French upheaval to that effect. One source of the inspiration for liberality was the recurrence to natural law that enabled the American Revolutionaries to counter the idea of parliamentary supremacy and provided the early French reformers with intellectual ammunition against the divine rights of kings. As one modern chronicler, Georges Lefebvre, of the French upheaval put it, "They gave voice to the rights of man and the citizen in their declarations of universal principles and they erected a republic in the name of the sovereignty of the people." Unfortunately, for all these declarations of principles, the "Reign of Terror" that followed the early reform years of the French Revolution exhibited the vengefulness that the Loyalists had escaped. *Rutgers v. Waddington* illustrated that difference—a lawsuit that began the reintegration of the losers in the civil war into civil society. A nation of courts and multitudes of lawsuits, not guillotines and basketfuls of severed heads, emerged from the first American civil war.

Was this American difference an example of American exceptionalism? The term itself is a controversial one. It was the aristocratic French visitor to the United States, Alexis de Tocqueville, who first coined the term, writing in his 1835 travel account that "The position of the Americans is therefore quite exceptional, and it may be believed that no democratic people will ever be placed in a similar one." The term gained its modern form under the hands of political scientist Louis Hartz, who found "national uniqueness" in the absence of a feudal past and an aristocracy, and sociologist Seymour Martin Lipset, who believed America made a virtue of individualism and rights, ingrained ideals largely absent from other nation states in their formative years. As Lipset wrote in 1997, "Being an American is an ideological commitment . . . an ism." A commitment in which "law is the only sovereign" was a core constituent of that "ism." Was legal forgiveness of one's former enemies another?

While the outcome and the legacies of *Rutgers* seem to lend support to this thesis, a more potent test of this example of this sort of American legalist exceptionalism is the conclusion of the second American civil war. Ironically, this civil war began with leaders of the Confederacy invoking the Revolution as precedent for secession. As the framers of the South Carolina secession ordinance wrote at the end of December 1860, "Thus were established the two great principles asserted by the Colonies, namely: the right of a State to govern itself; and the right of a people to abolish a Government when it becomes destructive of the ends for which it was instituted. And concurrent with the establishment of these principles, was the fact that each Colony became and was recognized by the mother Country a FREE, SOVEREIGN AND INDEPENDENT STATE." It was just this kind of argument in defense of absolute state sovereignty underlying the Trespass Act that Hamilton countered in his brief for Waddington.

With the lessons of *Rutgers* in mind, one can ask if the defeat of the Confederacy followed the historic pattern of revenge and reaction established in other civil wars or the precedent set by the end of the American Revolution? Although the conduct of the Civil War from 1861 to 1865 sometimes verged on criminality and included violence against neutrals and civilian populations, the peace did not feature wholesale reprisals. The winners did not impose crippling postwar debilities on the losers, but instead, after a relatively brief period of remarkably well controlled spite, made genuine efforts to reincorporate the losers into the Union. The case for comparison is obvious: Loyalists in New York were voting in state and city elections within a year after the war's end. Individual Confederates were pardoned within a year after the bloodletting ended upon taking an oath of loyalty, and in 1871 a general pardon ensued. The leniency federal authorities afforded to former Confederates was not in turn extended by them to their former bondsmen. Instead, the "redeemed" Confederates sought every means within the law, and sometimes outside of it, to effectually re-enslave the freedmen.

To explore this comparison one needs to begin where Hamilton began, with his application of the laws of war to the *Rutgers* case. Recall that he had seen the horrors of civil war firsthand. He also saw the possibility of humane treatment of prisoners, civilians under former enemies' control, and aliens affiliated with a former enemy. Finally, he argued that treaties could ameliorate former animosity as well as end open hostilities.

Hamilton's reading of passages from Vattel may not have been the inspiration for this effort—that was closer to home—and Vattel's moralism was at variance with Hamilton's realism. Thus his citation of Vattel in the later versions of the brief has a somewhat disjointed quality. Vattel was nevertheless as strong an authority for Hamilton's case as he could have found.

Vattel's basic premise was that "the law of nations is the law of sovereigns; free and independent states are moral persons, whose rights and obligations we are to establish in this treatise." Although in a civil war, "the entire nation is then obliged to maintain that association; and as their preservation depends on its continuance, it thence follows that every nation is obliged to perform the duty of self-preservation," the energy expended to maintain the nation need not lead to immoral acts when peace is achieved. "If a nation is obliged to preserve itself, it is no less obliged carefully to preserve all its members." These included former rebels.

The same moral imperative applied to the proper implementation of treaties. "As the engagements of a treaty impose on the one hand a perfect obligation, they produce on the other a perfect right. The breach of a treaty is therefore a violation of the perfect right of the party with whom we have contracted; and this is an act of injustice against him." With peace, whether by treaty or by the laws of war, "the enemy, in giving back a town at the peace, renounces the right he had acquired by arms. It is just the same as if he had never taken it; and the transaction furnishes no reason which can justify the sovereign in refusing to reinstate such town in the possession of all her rights, and restore her to her former condition."

Vattel concluded the third book of his *Laws of Nations* with a section on civil war that applied even more pointedly to Hamilton's argument in *Rutgers*.

> It is a question very much debated, whether a sovereign is bound to observe the common laws of war towards rebellious subjects who have openly taken up arms against him? A flatterer, or a prince of a cruel and arbitrary disposition, will immediately pronounce that the laws of war were not made for rebels, for whom no punishment can be too severe. Let us proceed more soberly, and reason from the incontestable principles above laid down.

Punishment of former rebels was not the conduct of a good or wise sovereign.

> Although it be his duty to repress those who unnecessarily disturb the public peace, he is bound to show clemency towards unfortunate persons, to whom just causes of complaint have been given, and whose sole crime consists in the attempt to do themselves justice: they have been deficient in patience rather than fidelity. Subjects who rise against their prince without cause deserve severe punishment: yet, even in this case, on account of the number of the delinquents, clemency becomes a duty in the sovereign.

If the treatment of the Loyalists after the Revolutionary War proved that Vattel's views were sound policy, then were they not right for Reconstruction after the next American Civil War?

Lincoln's chief advisor on the laws of war during the Civil War was Francis Lieber. As Lieber prepared a code for the conduct of Union Army forces during the war, he must have had open at his desk a copy of Vattel. Lieber did not slavishly copy the Swiss diplomat, but one cannot understand Lieber's thinking without measuring it (as he did) against Vattel. Lieber was a proponent of total war—a war that would crush the Confederacy, and slavery, so thoroughly that neither would rise again. He was, thus, not an advocate of Vattel's idealization of humane warfare. Vattel had argued that the property of private citizens in territory engaged in civil war should not be confiscated by the victor. That is what had made Vattel so attractive to Hamilton. Lincoln's Emancipation Proclamation, strongly supported by Lieber, was the very opposite of Vattel's proposal. Lieber wrote the rationale for that rejection of Vattel in what became Order 100.

But that order did not abandon Vattel's views on the peace that followed a civil war. For a year after the Emancipation Proclamation subjected confederate civilians to punishment of loss of their slaves, Lincoln issued his Reconstruction Proclamation. Like the former document, it was an attempt to legalize the conduct of the war, and terms of the peace. It was generous but more important it required a series of legal steps for the reintegration of a fractured society.

> Whereas, it is now desired by some persons heretofore engaged in said rebellion to resume their allegiance to the United States, and to reinaugurate loyal state governments within and for their respective states: Therefore— I, ABRAHAM LINCOLN, President of the United States, do proclaim, declare, and make known to all persons who have, directly or by implication, participated in the existing rebellion, except as hereinafter excepted, that a full pardon is hereby granted to them and each of them, with restoration of all rights of property, except as to slaves, and in property cases where rights of third parties shall have intervened, and upon the condition that every such person shall take and subscribe an oath, and thenceforward keep and maintain said oath inviolate.

Thrown with great force out the front door for the purposes of ending slavery, Vattel was welcomed at the back door for the purposes of restoring the Union.

What is more, as in both civil wars' close, instead of treating those who waged war against their former country with bills of attainder and other, state legislatures in 1784 and Congress in 1865 turned to the courts to administer the peace. When newly constituted (or reconstituted, depending on one's view of the rebellions) states acted in defiance of the spirit of the laws, legislative bodies passed more laws that gave to courts greater enforcement powers. Thus the rule of law was of paramount importance in settling the peace. To be sure, it was no accident that policies to insure good order that relied on courts were the work of lawyers in government. Lawyers dominated the process of peacemaking in the post war eras of 1783–1788 and 1865–1877. Even when the South was reoccupied by federal troops under congressional reconstruction, along with the troops came provost marshal courts and freemen's courts administered by Union Army officers. A legalistic nation found in law a way to reknit its parts.

At its farthest distance in time, *Rutgers* stood for something far more important than a widow's back rent, the former Loyalists' return to citizenship, the rise to prominence of Alexander Hamilton's ideas of national unity, the fair treatment of foreign businesses, or even the importance of treaties in American constitutionalism. It stood for a commitment to resolve differences, even the most virulent and violent of differences, under a rule of law. It stood for the autonomy of the judicial branch in a system of checks and balances. It stood for a basic sense of fair play. In 1784 and 1865, the sense of fair play had been sorely tested by civil warfare. But *Rutgers* and its legacy envisioned a polity in which former enemies could find neutral forums to resolve disputes and then willingly accept the decisions of these forums. To load all of this on one case in New York's Mayor's Court may seem overreaching, but at the time, contemporaries thought the case of great importance. If, in the course of nearly two and a half centuries of legal and political change, *Rutgers*'s significance has diminished, it is surely long past time to restore its place in the canon.

1764–1773	Protests against Parliamentary acts foster Whig opposition
1773–1774	Boston Tea Party and reprisal Boston Port Act lead to first Continental Congress. Alexander Hamilton arrives in Mainland colonies and matriculates at King's College in New York City. Committees of Fifty and Sixty form in NYC.
1775	Battles of Lexington, Concord, and Bunker Hill inaugurate open warfare between British regulars and colonial militia. Continental forces invade Canada. Committee of One Hundred forms in NYC.
June–September 1776	British forces depart Nova Scotia and defeat Continental Army in battles of Brooklyn and Manhattan. British army occupies New York City. Patriots flee NYC and Loyalists arrive from the countryside. Rutgers brewhouse used as barracks.
September 18, 1778	Commissary general issues license to Waddington and Pierrepont to operate brewhouse. Their agent, Joshua Waddington, lays out £700 for repairs to brewhouse.
May 1, 1780	Commander British forces orders Waddington to pay yearly £150 rent to poorhouse
November 30, 1782	Provisional treaty of peace signed
March 17, 1783	Trespass Act goes into effect over a stay by the Council of Revision
April 15, 1783	Provisional treaty ratified
June 30, 1783	British order Waddington to pay rent to Anthony Rutgers
September 3, 1783	Treaty goes into force without provision for mandatory reparations to Loyalists
November 23, 1783	Fire destroys brewhouse
November 25, 1783	Evacuation Day, final British occupation forces leave the city

January ?, 1784	First *Phocion* letter published anticipating many of Hamilton's arguments in the *Rutgers* briefs
February–March, 1784	*Mentor's Reply* published disputing arguments in *Phocion*
February 10, 1784	Sheriff brings Waddington to Mayor's Court
February 24, 1784	Mayor's Court session begins. Lawrence files pleading. Hamilton appears in court for Waddington.
February 24–April ?, 1784	Hamilton drafts briefs for *Rutgers v. Waddington*
April 1784	Second *Phocion* letter appears
June 29, 1784	Oral argument in *Rutgers v. Waddington*. Briefs submitted.
August 17, 1784	Duane delivers decision of court
August 27, 1784	Duane delivers opinion of court. Opinion published.
September 2, 1784	Jury finds damages of £791 for Rutgers
October 12, 1784	Lawrence files writ of error. Hamilton drafts brief for hearing in Supreme Court on writ of error.
November 2, 1784	Assembly debates censure of court and decision. No action taken on latter, and censure motion of Duane and Varick negatived.
July 5, 1785	Settlement negotiated in *Rutgers v. Waddington*. Case ends.
April 4, 1787	Portions of Trespass Act repealed
May–September, 1787	Constitutional Convention meets and drafts federal Constitution
June 18, 1787	Hamilton speech in constitutional convention
May 28, 1788	[Hamilton] Federalist Number 78 published
April 1792	*Rutgers* is the centerpiece of diplomatic correspondence between George Hammond, Alexander Hamilton, and Thomas Jefferson
March 7, 1796	*Ware v. Hylton* decided
February 24, 1803	*Marbury v. Madison* decided
July 11, 1804	Hamilton and Burr duel, Hamilton is mortally wounded and dies the next day
1920	*State of Missouri v. Holland*, 242 U.S. 416 (1920)

Note from the Series Editors: The following bibliographical essay contains the major primary and secondary sources the author consulted for this volume. We have asked all authors in the series to omit formal citations in order to make our volumes more readable, inexpensive, and appealing for students and general readers. In adopting this format, Landmark Law Cases and American Society follows the precedent of a number of highly regarded and widely consulted series.

This bibliography includes the sources consulted for present volume along with very brief sketches of some of the modern controversy surrounding the case. It is not intended to be comprehensive, but will point the reader in the direction of additional materials.

The depiction of the gutted Rutgers brewhouse is derived from the "Statement" of Benjamin Waddington, an affidavit, in *Rutgers v. Waddington*. He was one of the two British merchants who rented the brewhouse during the British occupation of New York City. It is reproduced in Julius W. Goebel, ed., *Law Practice of Alexander Hamilton* (New York: Columbia University Press, 1964), 1: 317–318. It is undated, but must have been made sometime in February 1784.

On taverns in the colonies and Revolutionary America, see Benjamin Carp, *Rebels Rising: Cities in the American Revolution* (New York: Oxford University Press, 2007), 62–99, quotation on page 77, and more broadly, David W. Conroy, *In Public Houses: Drink and the Revolution of Authority in Colonial Massachusetts* (Chapel Hill: University of North Carolina Press, 1995); Sharon V. Salinger, *Taverns and Drinking in Early America* (Baltimore: Johns Hopkins University Press, 2002); and David Waldstreicher, *In the Midst of Perpetual Feasts: The Making of American Nationalism, 1776–1820* (Chapel Hill: University of North Carolina Press, 1997). Colonial breweries are featured in Amy Mittelman, *Brewing Battles: A History of American Beer* (New York: Algora, 2008), 5–22. On the merchant classes in the colonial city, see Cathy Matson, *Merchants and Empire: Trading in Colonial New York* (Baltimore: Johns Hopkins University Press, 1997), and Serena R. Zabin, *Dangerous Economies: Status and Commerce in Imperial New York* (Philadelphia: University of Pennsylvania Press, 2011).

New York City's Loyalists in wartime fill the pages of the still useful Lorenzo Sabine, *Biographical Sketches of Loyalists of the American Revolution*, 2 vols. (Boston: Little, Brown, 1864). More recent accounts of the City in wartime are Edwin G. Burrows and Mike Wallace, *Gotham: A History of New York City to 1898* (New York: Oxford University Press, 1999), 191–287; Ruma

Chopra, *Unnatural Rebellion: Loyalists in New York City during the Revolution* (Charlottesville: University of Virginia Press, 2011); Richard M. Ketchum, *Divided Loyalties: How the American Revolution Came to New York* (New York: Holt, 2002); Philip Ranlet, *The New York Loyalists* (Knoxville: University of Tennessee Press, 1986); and Judith L. Van Buskirk, *Generous Enemies: Patriots and Loyalists in Revolutionary New York* (Philadelphia: University of Pennsylvania Press, 2000). Van Schaack's letter to Jay, and the reunion of the two men appear on pages 369–370 of *Divided Loyalties*. Farther afield, see Maya Jasonoff, *Liberty's Exiles: American Loyalists in the Revolutionary World* (New York: Knopf, 2012), and Mary Beth Norton, *The British Americans: Loyalist Exiles in England, 1774–1789* (Boston, Little, Brown, 1972).

The concept that the Revolution was a struggle among the great families is nothing new. It was broached by Carl Becker in *The History of Political Parties in the Province of New York* (Madison: University of Wisconsin Bulletin, 1909), and explored in Dixon Ryan Fox in *The Decline of Aristocracy in the Politics of New York* (New York: Longmans, 1919). Mary Lou Lustig, *Privilege and Prerogative: New York's Provincial Elite, 1710–1776* (Fairleigh Dickinson University Press, 1995), continued this line of inquiry.

A voluminous source of the handbills, pamphlets, and correspondence of the revolutionary period in New York is Peter Force, *American Archives: Documents of the American Revolution*, 9 vols. (Washington, DC: Peter Force, 1838–1853), online at American Archives, http://dig.lib.niu.edu/amarch/. Hamilton praised Congress in *A Full Vindication of the Measures of Congress from the Calumnies of their Enemies* (New York: Rivington, 1774). Samuel Seabury's "Letters from a Westchester Farmer" appeared as *Free Thoughts on the Proceedings of the Continental Congress* (New York: Rivington, 1774).

Firsthand accounts of the battle of New York appear in Henry P. Johnston, *The Battle of Long Island and the Loss of New York* (Brooklyn, NY: Long Island Historical Society, 1878). The Franklin-Howe conference is described in Walter Isaacson, *Benjamin Franklin: An American Life* (New York: Simon and Schuster, 2003), 318–322. Rutledge's letter to Washington is quoted in James Haw, *John and Edward Rutledge of South Carolina* (Athens: University of Georgia Press, 1997), 96. Tryon dances attendance on Howe in Ambrose Serle's diary, quoted in Paul David Nelson, *William Tryon and the Course of Empire: A Life in the British Imperial Service* (Chapel Hill: University of North Carolina Press, 1990), 146. The travail of the Continental Army prisoners in New York City is the subject of Edwin G. Burrows, *Forgotten Patriots: The Untold Story of American Prisoners during the Revolutionary War* (New York: Basic, 2008).

A valuable source for the treatment of Loyalists in the city during the war is the correspondence between the British commanders in chief based in New York City, particularly the Sir Guy Carleton Papers, PRO 30/55 on microfilm (30 reels); Great Britain, Colonial Office, New York, Original Correspondence, CO/1089–1090 (2 reels); Great Britain, Protocols of Treaties, 1782–1783 FO 93/1-2 (1 reel); all available at the David Library of the American Revolution, Washington Crossing, Pennsylvania. The guide to the Guy Carleton Papers for 1783 is volume 4 of Historical Manuscripts Commission, *Report on the American Manuscripts in Royal Institutions of Great Britain* (1909; rev. ed. Boston, 1972). The quotations are from the microfilms accompanying items catalogued on pages 27–28, 255–256, 359–360. On Guy Carleton's policy toward the refugee slaves, see Edgar J. McManus, *A History of Negro Slavery in New York* (Syracuse, NY: Syracuse University Press, 1966), 158–159, quotation on page 159. The travails and revival of Trinity Church after the Revolution are the subject of Elizabeth Mensch, "Religion, Revival, and the Ruling Class; A Critical History of Trinity Church," *Buffalo Law Review* 36 (1987): 470–477. She argues that Hamilton and Duane at the time of *Rutgers* were afraid that the legislature would seize the property of Trinity Church, of which both men were members, under the authority of something like the Trespass Act.

Statutes of the State of New York bearing on the Loyalists appear in *Laws of the State of New York, 1777–1784*, 2 vols. (New York: Albany, 1886). *The Votes and Proceedings of the Assembly of New York* were printed first in Kingston, NY, in 1777, then in Poughkeepsie, in 1778 and 1779, and, then in Albany, and then New York City. The journals of the two bodies through the confederation period are available in the Evans Early American Imprints Series. A handy contemporaneous compilation of the laws regarding Loyalists is *Laws of the Legislature of the State of New York in Force against the Loyalists . . .* (London: Reynell, 1786). The introduction and the headnotes in this collation make the case for the Loyalists' property rights in light of the Peace Treaty of 1783. Reading these statutes is not a task for the squeamish. Some ran to many pages, multiple sections, and very detailed provisions. They incorporated terms of art—jargon—from older law. One is grateful that the drafters did not introduce Law French or Latin, other than a few places, intending the law to be plain to the republican layman. The layman who entered the thicket of these statutes still had to be a brave soul. Robert R. Livingston's comment on the proposed legislation appears in Robert R. Livingston to John Jay, January 25, 1784, in Henry P. Johnston, ed., *The Correspondence and Public Papers of John Jay* (New York: Putnam, 1891), 3: 108.

On rent law, rent wars, and intercolonial strife over boundaries and rents, See Sung Bok Kim, *Landlord and Tenant in Colonial New York, Manorial Society 1664–1775* (Chapel Hill: University of North Carolina Press, 1978), and

Philip Schwarz, *The Jarring Interests: New York's Boundary Makers, 1664–1776* (Albany: State University of New York Press, 1979).

The Council of Revision stayed the Trespass Act, but the assembly passed it over the stay and Clinton signed it into law. The council's charter allowed it to consider every act passed and suggest revisions. The legislature could override the stay. Of the over 6,000 acts passed during its existence, from 1777 to 1821, the council objected to 128, and 17 were passed over its objections. See Alfred B. Street, *The Council of Revision of the State of New York . . . and Its Vetoes* (Albany, NY: Gould, 1859).

There are hundreds of biographies and special topical studies of Hamilton. Most useful for purposes here were James Flexner, *Young Hamilton: A Biography* (Boston: Little, Brown, 1978); Ron Chernow, *Alexander Hamilton* (New York: Penguin, 2004) (quotations in text from pages 5 and 12); Forrest McDonald, *Alexander Hamilton, A Biography* (New York: Norton, 1982), and Broadus Mitchell, *Alexander Hamilton* (New York, Macmillan, 1957), vol. 1. The *Phocion* letters and correspondence from this period appear in volume 3 of Harold Syrett et al., eds., *The Papers of Alexander Hamilton* (New York: Columbia University Press, 1962–1978), 3: 484–497 (first letter), 3: 530–558 (second letter). The letter to Gouverneur Morris, February 21, 1784, appears in 3: 513. Duane's letter to Hamilton on May 5, 1782 appears in 3: 88; Hamilton to Livingston on April 25, 1785, can be found in 3: 611. Hamilton's proposal to void all laws in violation of the Peace Treaty of 1783 appears in 4: 152. On Hamilton and New York State finances during the confederation period, see Thomas C. Cochran, *New York in the Confederation: An Economic Study* (New York: Empire State, 1932), 128–138, and Dan T. Coenen, *The Story of the Federalist: How Hamilton and Madison Reconceived America* (New York: Twelve Tables, 2007), 7–9. The doctrine of best use is explored in Morton Horwitz, *Transformation of American Law, 1780–1860* (Cambridge, MA: Harvard University Press, 1977), 63–139.

Aaron Burr, like Hamilton, has spurred a considerable body of scholarship. The Burr-Hamilton duel colors this literature, as do the Burr trials for treason, forcing historians to take sides. The danger lies in reading their relationship, and Burr's character, backwards from the duel and the trials in 1807 to the 1780s. Most favorable to Burr is Nancy Isenberg, *Fallen Founder: The Life of Aaron Burr* (New York: Viking, 2007), quotations from pages 2, 7, 91, 92, and 307, and least friendly is David O. Stewart, *American Emperor: Aaron Burr's Challenge to Jefferson's America* (New York: Simon and Schuster, 2011). One may also consult Herbert S. Parmet and Marie B. Hecht, *Aaron Burr: Portrait of an Ambitious Man* (New York: Macmillan, 1967), quotation in the present text from their page 17. The description of Burr is taken verbatim from my own *The Treason Trials of Aaron Burr* (Lawrence: University Press of

Kansas, 2008), 7. For the Burr legal correspondence and records, see Mary Jo Kline, ed., *The Political and Public Correspondence of Aaron Burr* (Princeton: Princeton University Press, 1983), 1: xxx–xxxii, and reel 13 of the Aaron Burr Papers at the David Library.

On Egbert Benson, see Wythe Holt and David Nourse, eds., *Egbert Benson, First Chief Judge of the Second Circuit, 1801–1802* (New York: Second Circuit, 1987), and William Kent, ed., *Memoirs and Letters of James Kent* (Boston: Little, Brown, 1898), 20–22. On James Duane, see Edward P. Alexander, *A Conservative Revolutionary: James Duane of New York* (New York: Columbia University Press, 1938), and Leo Hershkowitz, "Federal New York: Mayors of the Nation's First Capital," in Stephen L. Schecter and Wendell Edward Tripp, eds., *World of the Founders: New York Communities in the Federal Period* (Lanham, MD: Rowman and Littlefield, 1990), 25–46. George Clinton is well served by John P. Kaminski, *George Clinton: Yeoman Politician of the New Republic* (Lanham, MD: Rowman and Littlefield, 1993). Though Philip Schuyler was of a different and somewhat harder to fathom generation, see Don Gerlach, *Proud Patriot: Philip Schuyler and the War for Independence, 1776–1783* (Syracuse, NY: Syracuse University Press, 1987), and Bayard Tuckerman, *The Life of General Philip Schuyler, 1733–1804* (New York: Dodd, Mead, 1904). Brockholst Livingston appears in Cynthia A. Kierner, *Traders and Gentlefolk: The Livingstons of New York, 1675–1790* (Ithaca, NY: Cornell University Press, 1992). On John Jay, see Richard B. Morris, *Witness at the Creation: Hamilton, Madison, Jay and the Constitution* (New York: Holt, Rinehart, and Winston, 1985), and Walter Stahr, *John Jay* (London: Bloomsbury, 2005), quotes from Jay on pages 52 and 53. Robert Troup is the subject of Wendell Edward Tripp, *Robert Troup: A Quest for Security in a Turbulent New Nation, 1775–1832* (New York: Columbia University Press, 1973). On William Harper of Tryon County, see William W. Campbell, *The Border Warfare of New York during the Revolution, or The Annals of Tryon County* (New York: Baker and Scribner, 1849).

For information on lawyers in the revolution and subsequent years, see the introduction to volume 1 of the *Law Practice of Alexander Hamilton*; Paul M. Hamlin, *Legal Education in Colonial New York* (New York: New York University Law Quarterly, 1939); and Charles H. McIlwain, *The American Revolution, A Constitutional Interpretation* (New York: Macmillan, 1924), the classic work, which balanced the legal arguments of both sides. John Philip Reid, *The Constitutional History of the American Revolution* (Madison: University of Wisconsin Press, 1995), traverses much of the same ground but argues that the right and the law were on the side of the Revolutionaries. Lawyers found themselves in the middle of public scraps about qualifications for voting, even as they held elective offices. See, e.g., Ellen Holmes

Pierson, *Remaking Custom: Law and Identity in the Early Republic* (Charlottesville: University of Virginia Press 2011), 37–39; Lars C. Golumbic, "Who Shall Dictate the Law?: Political Wrangling Between 'Whig' Lawyers and Backcountry Farmers in Revolutionary Era North Carolina," *North Carolina Historical Review* 73 (1996): 56–82 (Maclaine quoted on page 56); Robert Ernst, "Egbert Benson: Forgotten Statesman of Revolutionary New York," *New York History* 78 (1997): 4–32 (Benson quote at page 9), and Peter Charles Hoffer, *Law and People in Colonial America* (rev. ed. Baltimore: Johns Hopkins University, 1998), 127–153.

The depiction of the City Hall is taken from Eric Homberger, *New York City: A Cultural History* (Northampton, MA: Interlink, 2007), 50–55.

First off the mark with a detailed history of the case was Henry B. Dawson's *The Case of Elizabeth Rutgers versus Joshua Waddington* . . . (Morrisania, NY, 1866). Dawson wrote a short introduction and republished the opinion James Duane gave in court on August 27, 1784, and later published as *Arguments and Judgment of the Mayor's Court in a Cause between Elizabeth Rutgers and Joshua Waddington* (New York: Loudon, 1784). Another old classic on the Mayor's Court and its counterparts is the treatment in Alden Chester and Edwin Melvin Williams, *Courts and Lawyers in New York* (New York: American Historical Society, 1925), 1: 257–626. William Potter, "Judicial Power in the United States" *Michigan Law Review* 27 (1928): 174–176, briefly discussed the case as an example of the judicial controversies arising under the confederation.

Dawson and Williams were followed by Richard B. Morris's edition of *Select Cases of the Mayor's Court of the City of New York, 1674–1784*, American Legal Records, volume 2 (Washington, DC: American Historical Association, 1935), and Morris by the four volumes of Julius Goebel, Jr., *The Law Practice of Alexander Hamilton* (New York: Columbia University Press, 1964–1980).

Morris discussed *Rutgers* in his introduction (pages 57–59) and reproduced the Duane opinion (pages 302–327). The edition itself came early in a career that would span sixty years and six dozen books and helped launch the American Legal Records project of the American Historical Association. Though small of stature, Morris was a giant in the history department at Columbia University until his death in 1989. A mentor to generations of historians at Columbia, in conversation Morris was a lively raconteur. In his volume on the Mayor's Court he selected cases to demonstrate that law from the bottom up reflected the needs and desires of the common man, the laborer, and the employer. His approach thus overlapped the concerns of lawyers, judges, and legislators in the era of the New Deal. Morris was a democrat with both a small and capital D, and his interest in the class struggle found its way into his collection. He was not, however, a lawyer, and what today would be called the social history of law interested him more than its arcane technicalities. On Morris and the project of the Select Cases, see Philip Ranlet, *Richard B. Morris and American History in the Twentieth Century* (Washington, DC: University Press of America, 2004), 21–24.

Morris's counterpart and sometime rival, Columbia Law School Professor Julius Goebel Jr., included many pages (219–491) on the case in the first volume of his *Law Practice of Alexander Hamilton*. Goebel was a pioneer in bringing early American legal history into the curriculum of his and other law schools. His meticulous scholarship and forceful manner made him a most formidable advocate of the proposition that local institutions were as important parts of our legal heritage as the great courts and famous jurists.

In the *Law Practice*, Goebel's introduction minutely described the nature of legal practice, the structure of the courts, and like matters up to the time that Hamilton entered the profession. Goebel was not interested in social mores or economic conflicts, but in the actual practice of the law, with the result that the volumes are more interesting to students of law rather than students of revolutionary and early national history. His reprint of Hamilton's "Practical Proceedings of the Supreme Court of the State of New York," for example, included annotation not only on matters Hamilton could not have known, but corrections when Hamilton got the practice wrong. On Hamilton's "Practical Proceedings" see Goebel, *Law Practice of Alexander Hamilton*, 1: 37–54 (introduction), 55–143 (document). On Hamilton and the writ of error, see *Law Practice*, 3: 97. Goebel thought that *Rutgers* "caused the greatest consternation" (291) because it came when the state legislature "was conducting further punitive measures against the Loyalists."

The very best summary of common law pleading in the colonies is David Thomas Konig's introduction to *Plymouth Court Records, 1686–1859* (Wilmington, DE: Glazier, 1978), volume 1. The classic contemporary account of common law reception was St. George Tucker, *Blackstone's Commentaries, with Notes of Reference to the Constitution and Laws of the Federal Government of the United States and the Commonwealth of Virginia* (Philadelphia: Birch and Small, 1803), 5 v. The modern classic is William E. Nelson, *The Common Law in Colonial America* (New York: Oxford University Press, 2008–2015), 4 vols.

The members of the Mayor's Court serving at the time can be found in the *Minutes of the Common Council of the City of New York, 1784–1831* (New York: Brown, 1917). Volume 1 begins with volume 8 of the manuscript minutes on February 10, 1784. The broadside attack on Duane's opinion appeared in September 17, 1784, *An Address from the Committee Appointed at Mrs. Vanderwaters* (New York: Shepard-Kollogh, 1784), 9, 11, 13. The assembly's debate on the censure of Duane appeared in the journal of the assembly, October 27, 1784, *Votes and Proceedings of the Assembly* (New York: Elizabeth Holt, 1784), 22–23.

On the comparative legal weight of colonial acts and colonial court decisions, see William E. Nelson, "A Response: The Impact of War on Justice in the History of American Law" *Chicago-Kent Law Review* 89 (2014): 1127. The book in question in my text and Nelson's response was Nelson's first volume of *The Common Law in Colonial America, Volume 1: The Chesapeake and New England* (New York: Oxford University Press, 2008), and the unnamed referee in the article of the work, calling for greater emphasis on the legislative activity of the colonial assemblies, was the author of the present book. For more on pleading in common law systems in the eighteenth century setting, see the classic work William Nelson, *Americanization of the Common Law: The Impact of Legal Change on Massachusetts Society, 1760–1790* (Cambridge, MA: Harvard University Press, 1975); and, for the Mayor's Court, Morris's *Select Cases,* 74–177. A short version of the long and detailed story is Peter Charles Hoffer, "History of American Law: Colonial Period," in Kermit L. Hall, editor in chief, *Oxford Companion to American Law* (New York: Oxford University Press, 2002), 364–374. On the Anglicization of American law and American courts in the eighteenth century, the classic work is John M. Murrin, "The Legal Transformation: The Bench and Bar of Eighteenth-Century Massachusetts" in Stanley N. Katz and John M. Murrin, eds., *Colonial America: Essays in Politics and Social Development* (3rd ed. Boston, Little, Brown, 1983), 540–572.

For a clear analysis of the relationship of natural law, common law, municipal law, and the laws of war, begin with William Blackstone, *Commentaries on the Law of England,* 4 vols. (Oxford, Eng.: Clarendon Press, 1765–1769), quotations from 1: 27, 28, 29, 30, and 60; and then turn to the illuminating essays in Mark W. Janis, *America and the Law of Nations, 1776–1939* (New York: Oxford University Press, 2010), 2–10, and David Lemmings, ed., *The British and Their Laws in the Eighteenth Century* (Woodbridge, Suffolk, UK: Boydell Press, 2005), quotation in text from Michael Lobban, "Custom, Nature, and Authority: The Roots of English Legal Positivism" ibid., page 30. The idea that colonial protests arose when Britain tried to turn the command of the state from theory into reality comes from David Thomas Konig, "Virginia and the Imperial State: Law, Enlightenment, and 'The Crooked Cord of Discretion,'" ibid., 206–229. Franklin's letter to Charles Dumas appears in Benjamin Labaree, ed., *The Papers of Benjamin Franklin* (New Haven: Yale University Press, 1982), 22: 287.

The dangers of a consonance of disparate texts were most pronounced in Edward Pearson, ed., *Designs against Charleston: The Trial Record of the Den-*

mark Vesey Slave Conspiracy of 1822 (Chapel Hill: University of North Carolina Press, 1999), on which see Michael Johnson, "Denmark Vesey and His Co-Conspirators," *William and Mary Quarterly* 3rd. ser. 58 (2001): 915–976. The comparison of Jefferson's and Hamilton's reading notes is adapted from Jay Fliegelman, *Thomas Jefferson, Natural Language, and the Culture of Performance* (Palo Alto, CA: Stanford University Press, 1993), 5–7 (diacritical marks).

The notion that an English constitution or an ancient English constitution controlled Parliament goes back to the eighteenth-century English "commonwealthmen" pamphleteers. See Caroline Robbins, *The Eighteenth-Century Commonwealthman* (Cambridge, MA: Harvard University Press, 1959). Further exploration of this idea of the ancient constitution and republican virtue appears in J. G. A. Pocock, *The Ancient Constitution and the Feudal Law* (rev. ed., Cambridge, Eng.: Cambridge University Press, 1987), and Gordon S. Wood, *The Creation of the American Republic, 1776–1787* (Chapel Hill: University of North Carolina Press, 1969). The argument is somewhat differently approached in Reid, *The Constitutional History of the American Revolution*, a counselor's case for concept as settled law.

On New York City economic growth and politics in this period see Michael Kammen, "'The Promised Sunshine of the Future': Reflections on Economic Growth and Social Change in Post-Revolutionary New York," in Manfred Jonas and Robert V. Wells, eds., *New Opportunities in a New Nation, The Development of New York after the Revolution* (Schenectady, NY: Union College Press,1982), 109–144, quotation on page 111; Cathy Matson, "Liberty, Jealousy, and Union," in Paul A. Gilje and William Pencak, eds., *New York in the Age of the Constitution, 1775–1800* (Rutherford, NJ: Fairleigh Dickinson University Press, 1992), 112–150, quotation from page 121; Kenneth R. Bowling, "New York City, Capital of the United States, 1785–1790," in Stephen L. Schecter and Wendell Tripp, eds., *World of the Founders: New York Communities in the Federal Period* (Albany: New York State Commission on the Bicentennial of the United States Constitution, 1990), 1–24, quotation on page 2. Elkanah Watson is quoted in Sidney I. Pomerantz, *New York: An American City, 1783–1803* (New York: Columbia University Press, 1938), 153. Many Loyalists remained in the city after the peace and Loyalist lawyers were readmitted to practice: Ernest Wilder Spaulding, *New York in the Critical Period, 1783–1789* (New York: Columbia University Press, 1932), 125, 130.

On the idea of politics as an affair of honor, see Joseph Ellis, *Founding Brothers: The Revolutionary Generation* (New York: Knopf, 2000), and Joanne B. Freeman, *Affairs of Honor: National Politics in the New Republic* (New Haven: Yale University Press, 2001).

The accounts of the Annapolis Convention of 1786 and Shays' Rebellion are taken almost verbatim from my *For Ourselves and Our Posterity: The Preamble to the Constitution in American History* (New York: Oxford University Press, 2012), 37–41. Sources of quotations appear in the endnotes for those pages.

James Iredell ("Elector")'s "Letter to the Public" appears in John M. Griffth, ed., *Life and Correspondence of James Iredell, One of the Justices of the Supreme Court* (New York: Appleton, 1858), 2: 145–149. Discussion of North Carolina's judicial politics in the confederation era is from Peter Charles Hoffer and N. E. H. Hull, *Impeachment in America, 1635–1805* (New Haven: Yale University Press, 1984), 88–91.

Hamilton's speech at the Constitutional convention appears in Max Farrand, ed., *Records of the Federal Constitution* (New Haven: Yale University Press, 1911), 1: 283–292, and my account of the speech appears in Preamble, 49–58. John Dickinson's comments appear in Farrand, ed., *Records* 2: 299, and Elbridge Gerry's comments appear in Farrand, ed., Records 1: 97. James Madison's "Observations" appears in J. C. A. Stagg et al., eds., *The Papers of James Madison: Congressional Series* (Charlottesville: University Press of Virginia, 1977–), 11: 285–293. Hamilton's contributions to the Federalist papers are easily found online at the Founder's Constitution, http://press-pubs .uchicago.edu/founders/.

George Hammond feels "put upon" in Stanley Elkins and Eric McKitrick, *The Age of Federalism: The Early American Republic, 1788–1800* (New York: Oxford University Press, 1993), 245. On Hamilton's role as Hammond's informant, see Julian P. Boyd, *Alexander Hamilton's Secret Attempts to Control American Foreign Policy* (Princeton: Princeton University Press, 1964). Justice Holmes speaks in *State of Missouri v. Holland*, 252 U.S. 416, 432 (Holmes, J.).

The literature on judicial review is vast and riven with controversy. The view that judicial review was an unconstitutional invention unites jurists on the left and right. See Erwin Chemerinsky, "In Defense of Judicial Review: The Perils of Popular Constitutionalism," *University of Illinois Law Review* (2004): 673–690. A defense of judicial review is William E. Nelson, Marbury v. Madison: *The Origins and Legacy of Judicial Review* (Lawrence: University Press of Kansas, 2000). For examples of "popular constitutionalism" and its attack on judicial review, see, e.g., Larry Kramer, *The People Themselves: Popular Constitutionalism and Judicial Review* (New York: Oxford University Press, 2004) and Joseph Fishkin and William E. Forbath, "The Anti–Oligarchy Constitution," *Boston University Law Review* 94 (2014): 101–127. But criticism of judicial review also comes from the right: see, e.g., Robert

Lowery Clinton, Marbury v. Madison *and Judicial Review* (Lawrence: University Press of Kansas, 1989).

On *Rutgers* as a way station on the road to judicial review, see Daniel Hulsebosch, "A Discrete and Cosmopolitan Minority: The Loyalists, The Atlantic World, and the Origins of Judicial Review," *Chicago-Kent Law Review* 81 (2006): 825–866, quotation at page 861; and Hulsebosch, *Constituting Empire: New York and the Transformation of Constitutionalism in the Atlantic World* (Chapel Hill: University of North Carolina Press, 2005), 196–200; William Michael Treanor, "Judicial Review Before *Marbury*," *Stanford Law Review* 58 (2005–2006): 455–562, especially 473–497, on the early state cases (but note that my reading of the precedential value of these cases differs from his); Goebel, *History of the Supreme Court of the United States: Antecedents and Beginnings to 1801*, vol. 1 of the *Holmes Devise History of the Supreme Court* (New York: Macmillan, 1971), 50–95, and Morris, *Select Cases*, 302. The "Prisoners' Case" (sometimes called the "case of the three prisoners") is *Commonwealth v. Caton*. 8 Virginia 1 (1782).

Was *Rutgers* in fact an example of judicial review? Contemporaries thought so, but later scholars, blessed with historical omniscience, demurred. It was not mentioned by the delegates in Philadelphia, but then again, they did not give to the courts the power of judicial review. See, e.g., William Crosskey, *Politics and the Constitution in the History of the United States* (Chicago: University of Chicago Press, 1953), 2: 965. Kramer, *The People Themselves*, 28, argues that *Rutgers* was not an example of judicial review at all, but merely statutory interpretation. The idea that judicial review is a shadow cast by a judge's duty to see statutes in a constitutional light appears in Philip Hamburger, "Two Paradigms: Judicial Review and Judicial Duty," *George Washington Law Review* 78 (2010): 1170–1171. Hamburger, in *Law and Judicial Duty* (Cambridge, MA: Harvard University Press, 2009), 346–356, calls *Rutgers* an example of "equitable" statutory interpretation, but this very old English concept did not make a safe crossing of the Atlantic. See John F. Manning, "Textualism and the Equity of the Statute," *Columbia Law Review* 101 (2001): 78–81. Indeed, it was only recent legal scholarship that rediscovered the doctrine and retroactively applied it to cases like *Rutgers* as well as other entirely modern issues. See, e.g., William N. Eskridge, "Should the Supreme Court Read *The Federalist* but Not Statutory Legislative History?," *George Washington Law Review* 66 (1998): 1301, 1318. It is true that Duane engaged in statutory interpretation, but that is true in almost all cases of judicial review that involve statutes. Striking down a portion of a state law, whether overtly or covertly, is not mere statutory interpretation.

Sometimes *Rutgers* is cited as an important precedent, then dropped. For example, the foremost modern work on the thinking of James Madison at the convention, Jack Rakove's *Original Meanings: Politics and Ideas in the Making of the Constitution* (New York: Knopf, 1996), 28, calls the decision a "seminal one" and does nothing more with it. Other accounts of the case, for example Clinton, in Marbury v. Madison *and Judicial Review*, 50 ("Hamilton's client ultimately won the case") and Kramer, *The People Themselves*, 65–66 (Duane opinion simply Blackstone's when it was exactly the opposite), simply get the facts wrong.

John Marshall's opinion in *Marbury v. Madison* appears in 5 U.S. 137 (1803). There is a large and growing literature that downgrades the significance and the originality of *Marbury's* claims and the scope of its version of judicial review. See, e.g., Michael J. Klarman, "How Great Were the 'Great' Marshall Court Decisions?," *Virginia Law Review* 87 (2001): 1111, 1113 and Jack Rakove, "The Origins of Judicial Review: A Plea for New Contexts," *Stanford Law Review* 49 (1997): 1039–1040. Much of this literature is engaged with more recent uses of judicial review, see, e.g., Christopher Wolfe, *The Rise of Modern Judicial Review: From Constitutional Interpretation to Judge-Made Law* (rev. ed. Lanham, MD: Rowman and Littlefield, 1994), a conservative critique revised to be a little more friendly, and Mark Tushnet, *Taking the Constitution away from the Courts* (Princeton: Princeton University Press, 2000), a liberal critique. Apparently the view of judicial review shifts with the use any particular majority of the U.S. Supreme Court makes of it.

The public/private law distinction is a much controverted idea, particularly when applied to continental law systems. For a sharply argued summary of the concept in its American context, see Morton J. Horwitz, *The Transformation of American Law, 1870–1960* (Cambridge, MA: Harvard University Press, 1992), 11–12, 26–27, 113–115, 165–166.

Francis Lieber's great tract on hermeneutics was his *Legal and Political Hermeneutics, or Principles of Interpretation and Construction in Law and Politics* (enlarged edition, Boston: Little and Brown, 1839), quotations at 39, 40, 48, 52, 56, 57, 59. Hamilton's plea for New York to enact a law repealing previous laws in conflict with the Peace Treaty of 1783 appears in Syrett, *Papers of Alexander Hamilton*, 4:150–152. His holding action at the New York State ratification convention is documented in Pauline Maier, *Ratification: The People Debate the Constitution, 1787–1788* (New York: Simon and Schuster, 2010), 320–400. On *Hamilton* and Ellsworth, see MacDonald, Hamilton, 290, and on the Judiciary Act section 25 and judicial review, see James A. Curry, et al., *Constitutional Government: The American Experience* (Dubuque, IA: Kendall Hunt, 2003), 121.

On the theory that the federal Constitution was the culmination of a counterrevolution, see Charles Beard, *An Economic Interpretation of the Con-*

stitution of the United States (New York: Macmillan, 1913); Merrill Jensen, *The New Nation: A History of the United States during the Confederation, 1781–1789* (New York: Knopf, 1950); Saul Cornell, *The Other Founders: Anti-Federalism and the Dissenting Tradition in America, 1788–1828* (Chapel Hill: University of North Carolina Press, 1999), and Woody Holton, *Unruly Americans and the Origins of the Constitution* (New York: Hill and Wang, 2007). On the idea that the basis of the Constitution is the protection of private property, see Jennifer Nedelsky, *Private Property and the Limits of American Constitutionalism: The Madisonian Framework and its Legacy* (University of Chicago Press, 1990); Madison, Federalist Number 10, quoted on page 17, and Morris, "Political Inquiries" [ca. 1800], quoted on page 68. To be sure, the thesis of counterrevolution has its critics. Perhaps the best of the more recent of these is Jack Rakove, *Revolutionaries: A New History of the Invention of America* (New York: Houghton, 2010), 396–444.

The source of the quotation comparing the American and the French Revolutions is Georges Lefebvre, *The French Revolution, From Its Origins to 1793*, tr. Elizabeth Moss Evanson (rev. ed. London: Routledge, 2005), 82. On American exceptionalism, see Louis Hartz, *The Liberal Tradition in America* (New York: Harcourt, 1955), quotation on page 4, and Seymour Martin Lipset, *American Exceptionalism: A Double-Edged Sword* (New York: Norton, 1997), quotations on pages 31 and 40.

A powerfully argued case for the Constitution as international law appears in David M. Golove and Daniel J. Hulsebosch, "Civilized Nation: The Early American Constitution, the Law of Nations, and the Pursuit of International Recognition," *New York University Law Review* 85 (2010): 932–1066. On Lieber, Vattel, and Order 100, see John Fabian Witt, *Lincoln's Code: the Laws of War in American History* (New York: Free Press, 2012), 170–285. For the reconstitution of a legal regime at the end of the war, see Harold M. Hyman, *A More Perfect Union: The Impact of the Civil War and Reconstruction on the Constitution* (New York: Knopf, 1973), 245–281, quotation at page 272.

Lamb, John, 5, 8, 25
  and battle for New York City, 12
Lansing, John, 103
Law of nations, 72, 77
  and constitution of New York,
    67, 79
  in *Rutgers v. Waddington*, 84
Lawrence, John
  biography of, 48–49
  files in *Rutgers v. Waddington*,
    57
Laws of war
  as applied to New York State,
    69
  and prisoners, 15
Ledyard, Isaac, 61
Lee, Charles, 11–12
Lewis, Morgan, 50–51
Lieber, Francis
  on civil wars, 128–129
  and interpretation of statutes,
    85
  and *Legal and Political
    Hermeneutics*, 85
  and Vattel, 128–129
Litigation, motives for, 44–45, 46
Livingston, Henry Brockholst, 39
  and *Rutgers v. Waddington*, 50
Livingston, Philip, 10
Livingston, Robert, 9
Livingston, Robert R., 32, 38
Livingston, William, 20
  on drunkenness, 2–3
Livingston Manor, 3
Loyalism, as civil disobedience, 27
Loyalist Code, 25, 27, 105
  and lawyers, 30
Loyalists
  and courts of law, ix
  departure of, 21
  and end of the war, 19
  lawyers among, 35
  in New York City, 9–12
  and occupation of New York
    City, 16

Madison, James
  at Annapolis conference, 100–
    101
  on Hamilton oration, 104
  on judicial review, 121
  on property, 124
Marbury v. Madison (1803), 113
Massachusetts Constitution, and
    supremacy of the legislature,
    76
Mayor's Court, 39, 41
  bench of, 46–47, 47–48
  and Loyalist cases, 41
  and New York City history,
    43–44
  pleading in, 56, 57
  and *Rutgers v. Waddington*, 45
McDougall, Alexander, 8, 25
Mentor's Reply to Phocion, 59–61
  authorship of, 61
Merchants
  British, 39, 51
  and British Empire, 22
  in New York City, 17–18, 96
Morris, Gouverneur, on property,
    124
Morris, Richard B., on Mayor's
    Court, 87, 135
  and legal history, 135
Myles Cooper, 4

Natural law, 54
Nelson, William, on colonial
    courts, 87
New Jersey Plan, 104
New York City
  brewing in, 2
  in British Empire, 7–8
  commerce in, 7
  and end of occupation, 23
  protests in, 8
  recovery of, 95–97
  in War for Independence, 12–22
New York Manumission Society,
    98

New York State
  constitution of, 24, 82
  lawyers in, 35–38
  legislature of, 24–25, 76–77
  opposition to *Rutgers v.
    Waddington* in, 91–93
  politics in, 32–33, 93
  sovereignty of, 60, 67, 70, 71–72

Oath of abjuration, 12

Pamphlets, of Revolution, 55
Patriots (Revolutionaries)
  in New York City, 10–12
Pendleton, Edmund, on judicial
  review, 75, 76
Pierrepoint, Evelyn, 5, 45
Politics in new nation, and *Rutgers
  v. Waddington*, 98–100
Preamble (to federal Constitution),
  108
Precedent, in common law, x, 74
Prisoners of War, after battle of
  New York, 15
Public law/private law distinction,
  85

Randolph, Edmund, on judicial
  review, 75
Reconstruction Proclamation, 129
Rent wars, 31
"Rule of law," 27, 129
Rutgers, Anthony, 45
Rutgers, Elizabeth (widow), 1
Rutgers brewhouse, 1
  burns, 45
  and occupation of New York
    City, 5, 6
Rutgers v. Waddington
  and Loyalist reincorporation, ix

Schuyler, Philip, 32
Seabury, Samuel, 11
Sears, Isaac, 5, 8, 25
Second Continental Congress, 24

Seditious Libel Act (1781), 29–30
Separation of powers, 82–83
Shays' Rebellion, 101–102
Slaves, in New York City, 18
Smith, Melancton, 40, 93, 96
Smith, William, Jr., 10, 11, 22
Sons of Liberty, 4, 5, 9
  in New York City, 8
Sovereignty
  and law of nations, 79
  of the people, 80, 90
  of states, 53–54, 92, 106–108,
    126
Stamp Act Congress, 44
State of Missouri v. Holland (1920),
    113
"States' rights," 123–124
Supremacy Clause (of federal
    Constitution), 108–109
Symsbury's Case (1785, CT), 114–
    115

Taverns, in colonies, 2
  and protests, 5
"Tea Party," 3, 9
Ten-Pound Cases (1786–1787, NH),
    115
Terms of art, 135
Treason, 29, 63
Treaty of Peace (1783), 108
  Article IV of, 34, 35
  Article V of, 34
  and Confederation Congress, 53
  and former Loyalists, 32
  news of, 20
  and New York State legislature,
    102
  reception in United States, 63
  and return of British property,
    21
Trespass, writs of, 56
Trespass Act (1783)
  described, 30
  and military necessity defense to,
    31–32, 64, 79, 80, 84, 85

Trespass Act (1783), *continued*
    and national politics, 108–109
    as remedial act, 78, 80
    and supremacy of the
        Confederation, 58
Trevett v. Weeden (1786, RI), 115
Trinity Church (New York City), 19
Troup, Robert, 48, 49
Tryon, William, 9, 12, 15
Tucker, St. George, on judicial
    review, 75

Union (of the states), 71, 107,
    109–110
    and opinion in *Rutgers v.*
    Waddington, 77

Varick, Richard
    biography of, 47
    and Mayor's Court, 46–47
Vattel, Emmerich
    on civil wars, 89, 128
    in Hamilton's legal briefs, 88–89
    and *Law of Nations*, x, 37
    on laws of war, 127–128
    and natural law, 89

Virginia Constitution, and
    supremacy of the legislature,
    76
Virginia Plan, 104

Waddington, Benjamin, 5, 45
Waddington, Joshua, 5, 45
Ware v. Hylton (1796), 113
War for Independence, ix
Washington, George
    and Alexander Hamilton,
        13–14
    and battle for New York City,
        11–12
    and end of occupation, 22
Wilcox, William, 49
Writ pleading, 56
Writs of error, 46, 81
Wythe, George, on judicial review,
    75–76

Yates, Abraham, 103, 104, 109
    on Hamilton oration, 104,
    107

Zenger, John Peter, 44